MILLER'S
ANTIQUES MARKS

MILLER'S ANTIQUES MARKS

Judith Miller

MILLER'S

Miller's Antiques Marks
by Judith Miller
First published in Great Britain in 2013 by Miller's,
a division of Mitchell Beazley,
imprints of Octopus Publishing Group Ltd.,
Endeavour House, 189 Shaftesbury Avenue, London WC2H 8JY.
www.octopusbooks.co.uk
www.octopusbooksusa.com

Ceramic and Glass Consultant: Steven Moore

Miller's is a registered trademark of Octopus Publishing Group Ltd.
www.millersonline.com

An Hachette UK Company
www.hachette.co.uk
Distributed in the US by Hachette Book Group USA,
237 Park Avenue, New York NY 10017, USA.
Distributed in Canada by Canadian Manda Group,
165 Dufferin Street, Toronto, Ontario, Canada M6K 3H6.

While every care has been taken in the compilation of this book, neither the publisher nor the
author can accept any liability for any financial or other loss incurred by reliance placed on the
information contained in this book. The author has asserted her moral rights.

ISBN 9781845337988

A CIP record of this book is available from the British Library and the Library of Congress.

Printed and bound in China

Publisher: Alison Starling
Head of Editorial: Tracey Smith
Editorial Co-ordinator: Katy Armstrong
Copy editor: Carolyn Madden

Chief Contributor: Julie Brooke
Proofreader: Jo Murray
Indexer: Hilary Bird

Art Director: Jonathan Christie
Designer: Ali Scrivens, TJ Graphics
Additional Design: Janis Utton
Illustrator: Anne Weyer

Senior Production Manager: Peter Hunt

Contents

INTRODUCTION

Marks are one of the collector's most important tools when it comes to identifying and dating antiques. Of course, it is important to understand that they should never be relied upon completely, as many have been copied or faked. What you should rely on is experience. Handle as many antiques as you can and learn to combine your knowledge of marks with the knowledge of how an authentic piece looks and feels.

This book contains information on silver, ceramics, glass, costume jewellery, dolls, teddies and toys. Obviously it would be impossible to print every mark that was ever used so we have chosen a selection of the most common marks that you will find.

In most cases, we have labelled each mark with the name of the factory or designer that used it, their location and dates of operation. Where possible we have then provided further information about when the particular mark shown was used. In some cases, such as silver and some glass and ceramics, it is possible to narrow down the date of a piece very specifically, due to the use of date letters or cyphers. These sections of the book are clearly laid out and labelled to help you with dating.

Miller's Antiques Marks should prove to be an invaluable companion when looking around antique shops, auction rooms, flea markets and car-boot sales. So, make sure you keep it with you to help identify those finds!

Judith Miller.

ACKNOWLEDGEMENTS

Ceramics and glass consultant:
Steven Moore
Senior Specialist at Anderson & Garland, Newcastle; ceramics specialist on the BBC's Antiques Roadshow.

The publisher would like to thank:
Conrad Biernacki, Bergmann Auctions, Lyon & Turnbull, Robert McPherson, Alan & Sue Poultney of Scarab Antiques, Woolley & Wallis, the Dublin Assay Office.

Image credits:
P.1 Tennants; p.3 Woolley & Wallis; p.7 Dorotheum; p.109 Hickmet Fine Arts; p.117 Woolley & Wallis; p.221 Leslie Hindman; p.255 Private Collection; p.267 James D Julia.

SILVER

Rococo Revival silver candelabra, by J C
Klinkosch & Robert Garrard, 58.2oz

Introduction

SILVER

- It is impossible to assess the purity of silver with the naked eye. To prevent heavily alloyed silver being passed off as purer silver, a process was developed to test the purity of all silver.

- In 1300, a mark was introduced. It was applied to silverwares tested for quality (assayed). The stamp, known as the 'King's mark', represented a lion's head. This was called a 'leopart' and has

  Leopard's head

  become the leopard's head of today.

- In 1327, the Worshipful Company of Goldsmiths began to enforce the assay laws. As assaying was carried out at Goldsmiths' Hall in London the mark was referred to as a 'hallmark'.

- Silversmiths were often reluctant to travel long distances to bring their wares for assay. Many ignored the law and sold their wares unmarked. A dishonest minority produced substandard wares. This threatened to undermine the guarantee and so, in 1363, the power to test precious metals was granted to mayors of all cities and boroughs.

- Prior to c1350, few makers had marked their wares with an identifying device.

- Makers' marks became compulsory in 1363 so silversmiths who produced substandard wares could be traced.

- The supervisor of the tests was re-elected annually, so, from 1478 in London, silver was marked with a different letter each year.

- When the alphabet was exhausted, either the style of the letter or the form of the shield background was altered, and the cycle began again. Other assay offices introduced similar date letter marks.

1721 *1741* *1781* *1801*

- In 1544, the Goldsmiths' Company introduced the lion passant mark. This gradually replaced the leopard's head as the sterling mark.

- The leopard's head became increasingly recognized as the London mark.

- In 1560, York began to use a mark that was half leopard, half fleur-de-lys. Other cities to adopt marks at an early stage were Exeter and Edinburgh.

- The Goldsmiths' guarantee of quality (the lion passant) was used by several provincial assay offices, including York, Newcastle, Chester and Exeter, in conjunction with the town mark.

MILLING & THE BRITANNIA SILVER STANDARD

- By c1660, the practice of 'clipping' – paring a minute piece of silver from the edge of coins – was rife. From 1697, the government issued coinage with a milled edge to prevent this. In order to render silver clippings useless to a smith, the silver standard was raised from 925 parts per thousand (92.5%) to a purer 958.4 (95.84%).

- This new standard was denoted by two new marks, which replaced the leopard's head and lion passant. These were the lion's head and the figure of Britannia. The new standard was called the Britannia silver standard.

Lion's head   Britannia

- The Britannia standard remained obligatory until June 1720, when the sterling standard was reinstated along with the old sterling marks.

- On 1 December 1784, a tax was imposed on silver. Intended as a temporary duty, it lasted for 106 years. A mark showing the sovereign's head signified payment.

George III   Victoria
1785–1820   1837–90

- From 1784 until 1890, five marks appeared on English silver (sterling, town, date, maker, sovereign's head). From 1891 to the present day, only four marks are used on most English silver of the sterling or Britannia standard (sterling, town, date, maker).

CONVENTION MARKS

- From 1 June 1976, some marks used at certain assay offices in the United Kingdom, Austria, Denmark, Finland, Ireland, Norway, Portugal, Sweden and Switzerland became legally acceptable under an international convention. These include a fineness mark, a sponsor's mark, a common control mark and an assay office mark.

Common control mark

- Marks for the common European silver standard of 800 and 830 parts per thousand are also included, but these are not approved standards for articles sold in Britain.

SILVER

THE HALLMARKING ACT OF 1973

● The Hallmarking Act of 1973 stated that each piece of silver must be stamped with a sponsor's mark (this has largely replaced the maker's mark and shows the person responsible for manufacturing the piece), a standard mark, an assay office mark and a date letter. The standard marks are now identical at all four British assay offices, except in the case of sterling silver, where the Edinburgh Assay Office uses a lion rampant in place of the lion passant.

SCOTTISH SILVER

● In 1457, a standard for silver of no less than 11 parts out of 12 (the equivalent of 916 parts per thousand) was set in Scotland. A maker's mark and the mark of the dene or deacon (the chief office bearer of his craft in a town) was also required. As the deacon would be an active gold- or silversmith, a piece of this date could appear to bear two makers' marks.

● By 1483, a guild system had been established and the town mark was in use.

Edinburgh 1485–

● In 1681, a cycle of date letters was introduced that remains in use today, and the deacon's mark was replaced by the assay master's mark.

● In Edinburgh, from 1759, the assay master's mark was replaced by the thistle. This was replaced by the lion rampant in 1975. Otherwise, from the mid 18thC, the duty marks and optional marks used in Scotland follow those used in England.

1759–1975

1975–

Edinburgh

IRISH SILVER

● In Ireland, from 1637, silver was marked with an assay mark depicting a crowned harp. This stamp was also used as a Dublin town mark 1637–1807.

Dublin

Hibernia

● After 1731, a stamp showing the seated figure of Hibernia was used as Dublin's town mark.

UNMARKED WARES

- A substantial number of wares made before 1900 are incompletely marked or not marked at all.

- A piece may be part of a larger set produced strictly to commission and marked only on one piece. Alternatively, it could be part of a multi-piece item; for example, a candleholder that would originally have been attached to an inkwell. Or it could simply be too small to mark.

IMPORTED SILVER

- The Customs Act of 1842 stipulated that all silver imported to Great Britain or Ireland was to be assayed and marked in a British assay office, a requirement to be back-dated to 1800. This means that Continental silver is sometimes stamped with Queen Victoria's head.

- From 1904, all imported silver had to be marked with the relevant standard in decimal – for example, .925 for sterling silver, .958 for Britannia silver. The Hallmarking Act of 1973 dispensed with the decimal point and, whereas British silver of the Britannia standard is stamped 958.4 (parts per thousand), imported silver is still marked simply 958.

DUTY DODGERS

- Following the imposition of the tax on silver from 1784 to 1890, a number of methods of avoiding the duty were developed. These methods of 'duty dodging' are seen as separate from the innocent alterations to silverwares, and from faking. Duty dodging had the sole purpose of avoiding paying the levy.

- One method involved the use of transposed hallmarks. A high-quality silver piece was sent to assay; the stamped area was then removed and inserted into a piece of inferior quality. Hallmarks were also transposed from small pieces to much larger items, as the silver duty was partly based on weight.

- The evidence of duty dodging can be hard to spot. One clue may be in the position of the marks, which tended to vary with fashion. For example, a Queen Anne coffee pot would usually be marked underneath the base, whereas an 18thC coffee pot would tend to be stamped on the rim.

- The marks on early silver spoons, from c1680 to 1690, were randomly applied and it was not until c1700 that marks began to be arranged in groups.

Active Assay Offices

ASSAY OFFICES

- There are now only five assay offices in Britain and Ireland: London; Birmingham; Sheffield; Edinburgh; and Dublin.

- Today, lasers are used to mark many items, especially flat pieces such as watch backs.

- Punches continue to be used to mark small items with curved edges such as rings.

- Since 1975 all the assay offices, apart from Dublin, have used an identical date letter system. This is shown below.

- Dublin Assay Office has its own system that works in a similar way to the British one (see pages 26–30).

1975	A	1983	I	1991	R	1999	Z	2007	h
1976	B	1984	K	1992	S	2000	a	2008	j
1977	C	1985	L	1993	T	2001	b	2009	k
1978	D	1986	M	1994	U	2002	c	2010	l
1979	E	1987	N	1995	V	2003	d	2011	m
1980	F	1988	O	1996	W	2004	e	2012	n
1981	G	1989	P	1997	X	2005	f	2013	o
1982	H	1990	Q	1998	Y	2006	g		

SILVER

LONDON

- As early as 1180, an association of goldsmiths existed in London.

- In 1327, the Worshipful Company of Goldsmiths was given the right to enforce the assay laws.

- Until 1378, all silver had to be taken to Goldsmiths' Hall in the City of London for testing.

- Silver of the required quality was marked with the leopard's head. As other assay offices were granted powers, this mark became associated with the London Assay Office.

- The leopard's head was surmounted by a crown between 1478 and 1821. Sometimes, between 1790 and 1820, especially on small articles, the mark was omitted altogether.

Year	Mark	Year	Mark	Year	Mark
		1618-19	a	1637-38	v
		1619-20	b	1638-39	a
		1620-21	c	1639-40	B
		1621-22	d	1640-41	C
		1622-23	e	1641-42	D
		1623-24	f	1642-43	E
		1624-25	g	1643-44	ff
		1625-26	h	1644-45	G
		1626-27	i	1645-46	K
		1627-28	k	1646-47	J
		1628-29	l	1647-48	L
		1629-30	m	1648-49	P
1598-99	A	1630-31	n	1649-50	M
1599-1600	B	1631-32	o	1650-51	R
1600-01	C	1632-33	p	1651-52	O
1601-02	D	1633-34	q	1652-53	P
1602-03	E	1634-35	r	1653-54	Q
1603-04	F	1635-36	s	1654-55	R
1604-05	G	1636-37	t	1655-56	
1605-06	h				
1606-07	I				
1607-08	K				
1608-09	L				
1609-10	M				
1610-11	N				
1611-12	O				
1612-13	P				
1613-14	Q				
1614-15	R				
1615-16	S				
1616-17	T				
1617-18	V				

SILVER

Year	Mark	Year	Mark	Year	Mark	Year	Mark	Year	Mark
	🐆 🦁	1674-75	R	1693-94	q	1711-12		1729-30	O
1656-57		1675-76	S	1694-95	r	1712-13		1730-31	P
1657-58	B	1676-77	T	1695-96	s	1713-14		1731-32	Q
1658-59		1677-78		1696-97	t	1714-15		1732-33	R
1659-60	B	1678-79	a	1697-98		1715-16		1733-34	S
1660-61	C	1679-80	b	1698-99		1716-17	A	1734-35	T
1661-62	D	1680-81	c	1699-1700		1717-18	B	1735-36	V
1662-63	E	1681-82	d	1700-01		1718-19	C	1736-37	a
1663-64	F	1682-83	e	1701-02		1719-20	D	1737-38	b
1664-65	G	1683-84	f	1702-03		🐆 🦁		1738-39	C
1665-66	H	1684-85	g	1703-04		1720-21	E	1739-40	d d
1666-67	J	1685-86	h	1704-05		1721-22	F	1740-41	e
1667-68	K	1686-87	i	1705-06		1722-23	G	1741-42	f
1668-69	L	1687-88	k	1706-07		1723-24	H	1742-43	g
1669-70		1688-89	l	1707-08		1724-25	I	1743-44	h
1670-71	N	1689-90	m	1708-09		1725-26	K	1744-45	i
1671-72	O	1690-91	n	1709-10		1726-27	L	1745-46	k
1672-73	P	1691-92	o	1710-11		1727-28	M	1746-47	l
1673-74		1692-93	p			1728-29	N	1747-48	m

Date	Mark	Date	Mark	Date	Mark	Date	Mark	Date	Mark
	👑 🦁	1766-67	L	1785-86	k	1804-05	I	1823-24	h
1748-49	n	1767-68	M	1786-87	l	1805-06	K	1824-25	i
1749-50	O	1768-69	N	1787-88	m	1806-07	L	1825-26	k
1750-51	P	1769-70	O	1788-89	n	1807-08	M	1826-27	l
1751-52	q	1770-71	P	1789-90	o	1808-09	N	1827-28	m
1752-53	r	1771-72	Q	1790-91	p	1809-10	O	1828-29	n
1753-54	ſ	1772-73	R	1791-92	q	1810-11	P	1829-30	o
1754-55	t	1773-74	S	1792-93	r	1811-12	Q	1830-31	p
1755-56	U	1774-75	T	1793-94	s	1812-13	R	1831-32	q
1756-57	A	1775-76	U	1794-95	t	1813-14	S	1832-33	r
1757-58	B	1776-77	a	1795-96	u	1814-15	T	1833-34	s
1758-59	C	1777-78	b	1796-97	A	1815-16	U	1834-35	t
1759-60	D	1778-79	c	1797-98	B	1816-17	a	1835-36	u
1760-61	E	1779-80	d	1798-99	C	1817-18	b	1836-37	A
1761-62	F	1780-81	e	1799-1800	D	1818-19	C	1837-38	B
1762-63	G	1781-82	f	1800-01	E	1819-20	d	1838-39	C
1763-64	H	1782-83	g	1801-02	F	1820-21	e	1839-40	D
1764-65	I	1783-84	h	1802-03	G	1821-22	f	1840-41	E
1765-66	K	1784-85	i	1803-04	H	1822-23	g	1841-42	F

Active Assay Offices – London

Year	Year	Year	Year	Year
1842-43	1860-61	1879-80	1897-98	1916-17
1843-44	1861-62	1880-81	1898-99	1917-18
1844-45	1862-63	1881-82	1899-1900	1918-19
1845-46	1863-64	1882-83	1900-01	1919-20
1846-47	1864-65	1883-84	1901-02	1920-21
1847-48	1865-66	1884-85	1902-03	1921-22
1848-49	1866-67	1885-86	1903-04	1922-23
1849-50	1867-68	1886-87	1904-05	1923-24
1850-51	1868-69	1887-88	1905-06	1924-25
1851-52	1869-70	1888-89	1906-07	1925-26
1852-53	1870-71	1889-90	1907-08	1926-27
1853-54	1871-72	1890-91	1908-09	1927-28
1854-55	1872-73	1891-92	1909-10	1928-29
1855-56	1873-74	1892-93	1910-11	1929-30
1856-57	1874-75	1893-94	1911-12	1930-31
1857-58	1875-76	1894-95	1912-13	1931-32
1858-59	1876-77	1895-96	1913-14	1932-33
1859-60	1877-78	1896-97	1914-15	1933-34
	1878-79		1915-16	1934-35

Year	Letter	Year	Letter	Year	Letter	Year	Letter
1946-47	(leopard's head marks)	1946-47	L	1958-59	c	1970-71	p
1935-36	u	1947-48	M	1959-60	d	1971-72	q
1936-37	A	1948-49	N	1960-61	e	1972-73	r
1937-38	B	1949-50	O	1961-62	f	1973-74	s
1938-39	C	1950-51	P	1962-63	g	1974-75	t
1939-40	D	1951-52	Q	1963-64	h	For 1975–2013 see page 12	
1940-41	E	1952-53	R	1964-65	i		
1941-42	F	1953-54	S	1965-66	k		
1942-43	G	1954-55	T	1966-67	l		
1943-44	H	1955-56	U	1967-68	m		
1944-45	I	1956-57	a	1968-69	n		
1945-46	K	1957-58	b	1969-70	o		

EDINBURGH

- A silver standard was established in Scotland in 1457.

- Silverwares bearing Scottish hallmarks survive from the mid 16thC.

- Scotland was not subject to the Britannia standard, but when the sterling standard was restored in England in 1720, the standard of silver was raised in Scotland to the same level of purity and a tax was also levied.

Year	Letter
1681-82	a
1682-83	b
1683-84	c
1684-85	d
1685-86	e
1686-87	f
1687-88	g
1688-89	h
1689-90	i
1690-91	k
1691-92	l
1692-93	m
1693-94	n

SILVER

Date	Mark
[castle mark] [B]	
1694-95	O
1695-96	P
1696-97	Q
[castle mark] [heart]	
1697-98	T
1698-99	S
1699-1700	t
1700-01	u
1701-02	w
1702-03	X
1703-04	Y
1704-05	Z
1705-06	A
1706-07	B
[castle mark] [EP]	
1707-08	C
1708-09	D
1709-10	E
1710-11	F
1711-12	G
1712-13	H
1713-14	I
1714-15	K
1715-16	L
1716-17	M
1717-18	N
1718-19	O
1719-20	P
1720-21	Q
1721-22	R
1722-23	S
1723-24	T
1724-25	U
1725-26	V
1726-27	W
1727-28	X
1728-29	Y
[castle mark] [AU]	
1729-30	Z
1730-31	A
1731-32	B
1732-33	C
1733-34	D
1734-35	E
1735-36	F
1736-37	G
1737-38	H
1738-39	I
1739-40	K
[castle mark] [GED]	
1740-41	L
1741-42	M
[castle mark] [EL]	
1742-43	N
1743-44	O
[castle mark] [HG]	
1744-45	P
1745-46	Q
1746-47	R
1747-48	S
1748-49	T
1749-50	U
1750-51	V
1751-52	W
1752-53	X
1753-54	Y
1754-55	Z
1755-56	A
1756-57	B
1757-58	C
1758-59	D
[castle mark] [thistle]	
1759-60	E
1760-61	F
1761-62	G
1762-63	H
1763-64	I
1764-65	K
1765-66	L
1766-67	M
1767-68	N
1768-69	O
1769-70	P
1770-71	Q
1771-72	R
1772-73	S
1773-74	T
1774-75	U
1775-76	V
1776-77	W
1777-78	X
1778-79	Z
1779-80	U

Date	Mark	Date	Mark	Date	Mark	Date	Mark	Date	Mark
[town mark]		1796-97	Q	1815-16	j	1834-35	C	1852-53	[mark]
1780-81	A	1797-98	R	1816-17	k	1835-36	D	1853-54	[mark]
1781-82	B	1798-99	S	1817-18	l	1836-37	E	1854-55	T
1782-83	C	1799-1800	T	1818-19	m	1837-38	F	1855-56	[mark]
1783-84	D	1800-01	U	1819-20	n	1838-39	G	1856-57	[mark]
[marks]		1801-02	V	1820-21	o	1839-40	H	1857-58	A
1784-85	E	1802-03	W	1821-22	p	1840-41	I	1858-59	B
1785-86	F	1803-04	X	1822-23	q	[marks]		1859-60	C
[marks]		1804-05	Y	1823-24	r	1841-42	K	1860-61	D
1786-87	G	1805-06	Z	1824-25	s	1842-43	L	1861-62	E
1787-88	G	1806-07	a	1825-26	t	1843-44	M	1862-63	F
1788-89	H	1807-08	b	1826-27	u	1844-45	N	1863-64	G
1789-90	IJ	1808-09	c	1827-28	v	1845-46	O	1864-65	H
1790-91	K	1809-10	d	1828-29	w	1846-47	P	1865-66	I
1791-92	L	1810-11	e	1829-30	x	1847-48	Q	1866-67	K
1792-93	M	1811-12	f	1830-31	y	1848-49	R	1867-68	L
1793-94	N	1812-13	g	1831-32	z	1849-50	S	1868-69	M
1794-95	O	1813-14	h	1832-33	A	1850-51	T	1869-70	N
1795-96	P	1814-15	i	1833-34	B	1851-52	U	1870-71	O

SILVER

Date	Mark	Date	Mark	Date	Mark	Date	Mark	Date	Mark
	[town marks]	1889-90	(h)	1907-08	B	1926-27	V	1945-46	ℱ
1871-72	P	1890-91	(i)	1908-09	C	1927-28	W	1946-47	2
1872-73	Q		[town marks]	1909-10	D	1928-29	X	1947-48	ℛ
1873-74	R	1891-92	(k)	1910-11	E	1929-30	Y	1948-49	ℐ
1874-75	S	1892-93	(l)	1911-12	F	1930-31	Z	1949-50	𝒯
1875-76	T	1893-94	(m)	1912-13	G	1931-32	𝒜	1950-51	𝒰
1876-77	U	1894-95	(n)	1913-14	H	1932-33	ℬ	1951-52	𝒱
1877-78	V	1895-96	(o)	1914-15	I	1933-34	𝒞	1952-53	𝒲
1878-79	W	1896-97	(p)	1915-16	K	1934-35	𝒟	1953-54	𝒳
1879-80	X	1897-98	(q)	1916-17	L	1935-36	ℰ	1954-55	𝒴
1880-81	Y	1898-99	(r)	1917-18	M	1936-37	ℱ	1955-56	𝒵
1881-82	Z	1899-1900	(s)	1918-19	N	1937-38	𝒢	1956-57	A
1882-83	(a)	1900-01	(t)	1919-20	O	1938-39	ℋ	1957-58	B
1883-84	(b)	1901-02	(u)	1920-21	P	1939-40	𝒥	1958-59	C
1884-85	(c)	1902-03	(w)	1921-22	Q	1940-41	𝒦	1959-60	D
1885-86	(d)	1903-04	(r)	1922-23	R	1941-42	ℒ	1960-61	E
1886-87	(e)	1904-05	(y)	1923-24	S	1942-43	ℳ	1961-62	F
1887-88	(f)	1905-06	(3)	1924-25	T	1943-44	𝒩	1962-63	G
1888-89	(g)	1906-07	A	1925-26	U	1944-45	𝒪	1963-64	H

1964-65	🅰	*1970-71*	🅿
1965-66	🅱	*1971-72*	🆀
1966-67	🆂	*1972-73*	🆁
1967-68		*1973-74*	🆂
1968-69		For 1975–2013 see page 12	
1969-70			

BIRMINGHAM

- Assay office active since 1773.

- Mark is an anchor and is usually accompanied by a lion passant, a date letter, a duty mark (the sovereign's head) and the maker's initials.

- Today it is the largest assay office in the world and handles more than 12 million items made from precious metals every year.

	🦁⚓			*1788-89*	Q	*1799-1800*	b
		1778-79	F	*1789-90*	R	*1800-01*	c
1773-74	A	*1779-80*	G	*1790-91*	S	*1801-02*	d
1774-75	B	*1780-81*	H	*1791-92*	T	*1802-03*	e
1775-76	C	*1781-82*	I	*1792-93*	U	*1803-04*	f
1776-77	D	*1782-83*	K	*1793-94*	V	*1804-05*	g
1777-78	E	*1783-84*	L	*1794-95*	W	*1805-06*	h
	🦁⚓👑	*1784-85*	M	*1795-96*	X	*1806-07*	i
		1785-86	N	*1796-97*	Y	*1807-08*	J
	🦁⚓👑	*1786-87*	O	*1797-98*	Z	*1808-09*	k
		1787-88	P	*1798-99*	a	*1809-10*	l

SILVER

Year	Mark	Year	Mark	Year	Mark	Year	Mark	Year	Mark
	[lion/anchor/bust marks]	1828-29	E	1846-47	X	1865-66	Q	1884-85	k
1810-11	m	1829-30	F	1847-48	Y	1866-67	R	1885-86	l
1811-12	n	1830-31	G	1848-49	Z	1867-68	S	1886-87	m
1812-13	o	1831-32	H	1849-50	A	1868-69	T	1887-88	n
1813-14	p	1832-33	J	1850-51	B	1869-70	U	1888-89	o
1814-15	q	1833-34	K	1851-52	C	1870-71	V	1889-90	p
1815-16	r	1834-35	L	1852-53	D	1871-72	W		[lion/anchor marks]
1816-17	s	1835-36	M	1853-54	E	1872-73	X	1890-91	q
1817-18	t	1836-37	N	1854-55	F	1873-74	Y	1891-92	r
1818-19	u	1837-38	O	1855-56	G	1874-75	z	1892-93	s
1819-20	v		[lion/anchor/bust marks]	1856-57	H	1875-76	a	1893-94	t
1820-21	w	1838-39	P	1857-58	I	1876-77	b	1894-95	u
1821-22	x	1839-40	Q	1858-59	J	1877-78	c	1895-96	v
1822-23	y	1840-41	R	1859-60	K	1878-79	d	1896-97	w
1823-24	Z	1841-42	S	1860-61	L	1879-80	e	1897-98	x
1824-25	A	1842-43	T	1861-62	M	1880-81	f	1898-99	y
1825-26	B	1843-44	U	1862-63	N	1881-82	g	1899-1900	z
1826-27	C	1844-45	V	1863-64	O	1882-83	h	1900-01	a
1827-28	D	1845-46	W	1864-65	P	1883-84	i	1901-02	b

SILVER

⚓🦁	1917-18 S	1933-34 J	1949-50 Z	1965-66 𝔷
1902-03 c	1918-19 t	1934-35 K	1950-51 𝒜	1966-67 𝑅
1903-04 d	1919-20 u	1935-36 L	1951-52 ℬ	1967-68 𝑆
1904-05 e	1920-21 v	1936-37 M	1952-53 𝒞	1968-69 𝑇
1905-06 f	1921-22 w	1937-38 N	1953-54 𝒟	1969-70 𝑢
1906-07 g	1922-23 x	1938-39 O	1954-55 ℰ	1970-71 𝑉
1907-08 h	1923-24 y	1939-40 P	1955-56 ℱ	1971-72 𝑊
1908-09 i	1924-25 z	1940-41 Q	1956-57 𝒢	1972-73 𝑋
1909-10 k	1925-26 A	1941-42 R	1957-58 𝐻	1973-74 𝑌
1910-11 l	1926-27 B	1942-43 S	1958-59 𝒥	1974 𝑍
1911-12 m	1927-28 C	1943-44 T	1959-60 𝒦	For 1975–2013 see page 12
1912-13 n	1928-29 D	1944-45 U	1960-61 𝐿	
1913-14 o	1929-30 E	1945-46 V	1961-62 𝑀	
1914-15 p	1930-31 F	1946-47 W	1962-63 𝒩	
1915-16 q	1931-32 G	1947-48 X	1963-64 𝒪	
1916-17 r	1932-33 H	1948-49 Y	1964-65 𝑃	

For 1975–2013 see page 12

SILVER

SHEFFIELD

- By the middle of the 18thC, Sheffield was a major manufacturing centre for silver.

- The efforts of Matthew Boulton, a Birmingham industrialist, led to the Act of Parliament in which Sheffield was established as an assay office in 1773.

- Until 1974, Sheffield's mark depicted a crown, which featured along with the marks used at other assay offices.

- From 1975 the Tudor rose mark was used.

- Date letters were first used in 1773, starting with E, and changed irregularly each year until 1824. After this date the letters were arranged in alphabetical order.

Year	Letter	Year	Letter	Year	Letter	Year	Letter
	(crown & rose marks)	1781-82	D	1788-89	(mark)	1797-98	X
1773-74	E	1782-83	G	1789-90	(mark)	1798-99	V
1774-75	F	1783-84	B	1790-91	L	1799-1800	E
1775-76	P	(lion, crown, rose marks) 1784-85		1791-92	P	1800-01	N
1776-77	R	1784-85	J	1792-93	U	1801-02	H
1777-78	h	1785-86	V	1793-94	O	1802-03	M
1778-79	S	1786-87	k	1794-95	M	1803-04	F
1779-80	A	(lion, crown, rose marks) 1795-96		1795-96	q	1804-05	G
1780-81	Z	1787-88	L	1796-97	Z	1805-06	B
						1806-07	A
						1807-08	S
						1808-09	P
						1809-10	K
						1810-11	L
						1811-12	C
						1812-13	D
						1813-14	R
						1814-15	W
						1815-16	O
1816-17	T	1825-26	b				
1817-18	X	1826-27	c				
1818-19	I	1827-28	d				
1819-20	V	1828-29	e				
1820-21	Q	1829-30	f				
1821-22	Y	1830-31	g				
1822-23	Z	1831-32	h				
1823-24	U	1832-33	k				
1824-25	a	1833-34	l				
		1834-35	m				

Date	Mark	Date	Mark	Date	Mark	Date	Mark	Date	Mark
[crown / rose / shield marks]		1851-52	H	1870-71	C	1889-90	W	1907-08	p
1835-36	P	1852-53	I	1871-72	D	[rose / lion marks]		1908-09	q
1836-37	q	1853-54	K	1872-73	E	1890-91	X	1909-10	r
1837-38	r	1854-55	L	1873-74	F	1891-92	Y	1910-11	s
1838-39	S	1855-56	M	1874-75	G	1892-93	Z	1911-12	t
1839-40	t	1856-57	N	1875-76	H	1893-94	a	1912-13	u
[crown / rose / shield marks]		1857-58	O	1876-77	J	1894-95	b	1913-14	v
1840-41	u	1858-59	P	1877-78	K	1895-96	c	1914-15	w
1841-42	v	1859-60	R	1878-79	L	1896-97	d	1915-16	x
1842-43	X	1860-61	S	1879-80	M	1897-98	e	1916-17	y
1843-44	Z	1861-62	T	1880-81	N	1898-99	f	1917-18	z
[rose / crown / shield marks]		1862-63	U	1881-82	O	1899-1900	g	1918-19	a
1844-45	A	1863-64	V	1882-83	P	1900-01	h	1919-20	b
1845-46	B	1864-65	W	1883-84	Q	1901-02	i	1920-21	c
1846-47	C	1865-66	X	1884-85	R	1902-03	k	1921-22	d
1847-48	D	1866-67	Y	1885-86	S	1903-04	l	1922-23	e
1848-49	E	1867-68	Z	1886-87	T	1904-05	m	1923-24	f
1849-50	F	1868-69	A	1887-88	U	1905-06	n	1924-25	g
1850-51	G	1869-70	B	1888-89	V	1906-07	o	1925-26	h

(crown marks)	1936-37 t	1947-48 E	1958-59 Q	1969-70 B
1926-27 i	1937-38 u	1948-49 F	1959-60 R	1970-71 C
1927-28 k	1938-39 v	1949-50 G	1960-61 S	1971-72 D
1928-29 l	1939-40 w	1950-51 H	1961-62 T	1972-73 E
1929-30 m	1940-41 x	1951-52 I	1962-63 U	1973-75 F
1930-31 n	1941-42 y	1952-53 K	1963-64 V	1974 G
1931-32 o	1942-43 z	1953-54 L	1964-65 W	For 1975–2013 see page 12
1932-33 p	1943-44 A	1954-55 M	1965-66 X	
1933-34 q	1944-45 B	1955-56 N	1966-67 Y	
1934-35 r	1945-46 C	1956-57 O	1967-68 Z	
1935-36 s	1946-47 D	1957-58 P	1968-69 A	

DUBLIN

- Although Dublin's city council decreed that silver of the correct standard (coin) was to be marked with a lion, a harp and a castle, Irish silver was only sporadically marked.

- In 1637, a crowned harp and date letter was introduced, along with a maker's mark system.

- In 1731, the figure of Hibernia was introduced, and in 1807 the monarch's head was added as the duty mark, giving Dublin five marks until 1890, when the monarch's head was again dropped.

(crowned harp mark)		1645-46	H
1638-39	Æ	1646-47	I
1639-40	B	1647-48	K
1640-41	C	1648-49	L
1641-42	D	1649-50	M
1642-43	E	1650-51	N
1643-44	F	1651-52	O
1644-45	G	1652-53	P

Date	Letter	Date	Letter	Date	Letter	Date	Letter	Date	Letter
	(crowned harp)	1669-70	m	1699-1700	B	1724-25	E	1743-44	X
1653-54	Q	1670-71	n	1701-02	D	1725-26	F	1745	Y
1654-55	R	1671-72	o	1702-03	P	1726-27	G	1746	Z
1655-56	S	1672-73	p	1703-04	D	1727-28	H		(two marks)
1656-57	T	1673-74	q	1704-05	R	1728-29	I	1747	A
1657-58	U	1674-75	r	1706-07	S	1729-30	K	1748	B
1658-59	a	1675-76	s	1708-09	T	1730-31	L	1749	C
	(two marks)	1676-77	t	1710-11	(mark)		(two marks)	1750	D
1659-60	b	1677-78	u	1712-13	(mark)	1731-32	L	1751-52	EE
1660-61	c	1678-79	A	1714-15	X	1732-33	M	1752-53	F
1661-62	d	1679-80	B	1715-16	Y	1733-34	N	1753-54	G
1662-63	e	1680-81	C	1716-17	Z	1734-35	O	1754-56	H
	(mark)	1681-82	D	1717-18	a	1735-36	P	1757	U
1663-64	f	1682-83	E	1718-19	R	1736-37	Q	1758	K
1664-65	g	1683-84	F	1719-20	C	1737-38	R	1759	L
1665-66	h	1685-87	G	1720-21	A	1738-39	S	1760	M
1666-67	i	1688-93	H	1721-22	B	1739-40	T	1761	N
1667-68	k	1694-95	K	1722-23	C	1740-41	U	1762	O
1668-69	l	1696-99	L	1723-24	D	1741-43	W	1763	P

SILVER

Year	Mark	Year	Mark	Year	Mark	Year	Mark	Year	Mark
	🐦 🛡	1782	K	1801	E	1819	Y	1836-37	QQ
1764	Q	1783	L	1802	F	1820	Z	1837-38	RR
1765	R	1784	M	1803	G	1821	A		🦁 👤 👑
1766	S	1785	N	1804	H		👤	1838-39	S
1767	T	1786	O	1805	I	1822	B	1839-40	T
1768	U	1787	P	1806	K	1823	C	1840-41	UU
1769	W	1788	Q		🦁 🦅 💀	1824	D	1841-42	V
1770	X	1789	R	1807	L	1825-26	EE	1842-43	W
1771	Y	1790	S	1808	M	1826-27	F	1843-44	X
1772	Z	1791	T	1809	NN	1827-28	G	1844-45	Y
1773	A	1792	U	1810	OO	1828-29	H	1845-46	Z
1774	B	1793	W	1811	P	1829-30	II	1846-47	a
1775	C	1794	X	1812	Q	1830-31	K	1847-48	b
1776	D	1795	Y	1813	R		🦁 🦅 💀	1848-49	C
1777	E	1796	Z	1814	S	1831-32	L	1849-50	d
1778	F	1797	A	1815	T	1832-33	M	1850-51	e
1779	G	1798	B	1816	U	1833-34	NN	1851-52	ff
1780	H	1799	C	1817	W	1834-35	OO	1852-53	gg
1781	I	1800	D	1818	X	1835-36	PP	1853-54	hh

Date	Letter		Date	Letter		Date	Letter		Date	Letter
	🔲🔲🔲			🔲🔲		1908-09	𝕬		1927	𝖒
1854-55	j		1872-73	B		1909-10	𝕭		1928	𝖓
1855-56	k		1873-74	C		1890-91	U		1910-11	𝕯		1929	𝖔
1856-57	l		1874-75	D		1891-92	V		1911-12	𝕮		1930	𝖕
1857-58	m		1875-76	E		1892-93	W		1912-13	𝕽			
1858-59	n		1876-77	F		1893-94	X		1913-14	𝕾		Up to 1931 the date letter was changed on 1 June. The Q of 1932 began on 1 January	
1859-60	o		1877-78	G		1894-95	Y		1914-15	𝕿			
1860-61	p		1878-79	H		1895-96	Z		1915-16	𝖀			
1861-62	q		1879-80	U		1896-97	𝕬		1916	𝔄		1932	𝕼
1862-63	r		1880-81	K		1897-98	𝕭		1917	𝔟		1933	𝕽
1863-64	s		1881-82	L		1898-99	𝕮		1918	𝔠		1934	𝕾
1864-65	t		1882-83	M		1899-1900	𝕭		1919	𝔡		1935	𝕿
1865-66	u		1883-84	N		1900-01	𝕰		1920	𝔢		1936	𝖀
1866-67	v		1884-85	O		1901-02	𝕱		1921	𝔣		1937	𝖁
1867-68	w		1885-86	P		1902-03	𝕲		1922	𝔖		1938	𝖂
1868-69	x		1886-87	Q		1903-04	𝕳		1923	𝔥		1939	𝖃
1869-70	y		1887-88	R		1904-05	𝕵		1924	𝔦		1940	𝖄
1870-71	z		1888-89	S		1905-06	𝕶		1925	𝔨		1941	𝖅
1871-72	A		1889-90	T		1906-07	𝕷		1926	𝔩		1942	A
						1907-08	𝕸					1943	B
												1944	C

29

SILVER

Year	Mark	Year	Mark	Year	Mark	Year	Mark
	(two symbols)	1963	V	1982	R	2001	Q
1945	D	1964	W	1983	S	2002	R
1946	E	1965	X	1984	C	2003	S
1947	F	1966	Y	1985	U	2004	T
1948	G	1967	Z	1986	A	2005	U
1949	H	1968	a	1987	B	2006	V
1950	I	1969	b	1988	C	2007	W
1951	J	1970	c	1989	D	2008	X
1952	K	1971	d	1990	E	2009	Y
1953	L	1972	e	1991	F	2010	Z
1954	M	1973	f	1992	G	2011	A
1955	N	1974	g	1993	H	2012	B
1956	O	1975	h	1994	I	2013	C
1957	P	1976	i	1995	J		
1958	Q	1977	l	1996	K		
1959	R	1978	m	1997	L		
1960	S	1979	n	1998	M		
1961	T	1980	o	1999	N		
1962	U	1981	p	2000	O		

INACTIVE ASSAY OFFICES

EXETER

- The earliest Exeter assay mark dates back to the mid 16thC.
- Assay marking in Exeter was erratic until c1700.
- The assay office closed in 1883.

Year	Mark	Year	Mark	Year	Mark	Year	Mark
	🛡🛡🛡	1714-15	O	1727-28	C	1741-42	r
1701-02	A	1715-16	P	1728-29	d	1742-43	S
1702-03	B	1716-17	Q	1729-30	e	1743-44	t
1703-04	C	1717-18	R	1730-31	f	1744-45	u
1704-05	D	1718-19	S	1731-32	g	1745-46	w
1705-06	E	1719-20	T	1732-33	h	1746-47	x
1706-07	F		🛡🛡🛡	1733-34	t	1747-48	y
1707-08	G	1720-21	V	1734-35	k	1748-49	z
1708-09	H	1721-22	W	1735-36	l	1749-50	A
1709-10	I	1722-23	X	1736-37	m	1750-51	B
1710-11	K	1723-24	Y	1737-38	n	1751-52	C
1711-12	L	1724-25	Z	1738-39	o	1752-53	D
1712-13	M	1725-26	a	1739-40	p	1753-54	E
1713-14	N	1726-27	b	1740-41	q	1754-55	F
						1755-56	G
						1756-57	H
						1757-58	I
						1758-59	K
						1759-60	L

Year	Mark
1760-61	M
1761-62	N
1762-63	O
1763-64	P
1764-65	Q
1765-66	R
1766-67	S
1767-68	T
1768-69	U
1769-70	W
1770-71	X
1771-72	Y
1772-73	Z
1773-74	A
1774-75	B
1775-76	C
1776-77	D
1777-78	E
1778-79	F

SILVER

Leopard's head was not used after 1779		1795-96	X	1814-15	S	1833-34	T	1851-52	D
		1796-97	Y	1815-16	T	1834-35	S	1852-53	
1779-80	G	1797-98	A	1816-17	U	1835-36	t	1853-54	R
1780-81	H	1798-99	B	1817-18	a	1836-37	u	1854-55	S
1781-82	I	1799-1800	C	1818-19	b	1837-38	A	1855-56	T
1782-83	J	1800-01	D	1819-20	c	1838-39	B	1856-57	
1783-84	K	1801-02	E	1820-21	d	1839-40	C	1857-58	A
1784-85	L	1802-03	F	1821-22	e	1840-41	D	1858-59	B
1785-86	M	1803-04	G	1822-23	f	1841-42	E	1859-60	C
1786-87	N	1804-05	H	1823-24	g	1842-43	F	1860-61	D
		1805-06	I	1824-25	h	1843-44	G	1861-62	E
1787-88	O	1806-07	K	1825-26	i	1844-45	H	1862-63	F
1788-89	P	1807-08	L	1826-27	k	1845-46	I	1863-64	G
1789-90	q	1808-09	M	1827-28	l	1846-47	K	1864-65	H
1790-91	r	1809-10	N	1828-29	m	1847-48	L	1865-66	I
1791-92	s	1810-11	O	1829-30	n	1848-49	M	1866-67	K
1792-93	t	1811-12	P	1830-31	o	1849-50	N	1867-68	L
1793-94	u	1812-13	Q	1831-32	p	1850-51	O	1868-69	M
1794-95	W	1813-14	R	1832-33	q			1869-70	N

SILVER

Date	Letter
1870-71	Ⓞ
1871-72	Ⓟ
1872-73	Ⓠ
1873-74	Ⓡ
1874-75	Ⓢ
1875-76	Ⓣ
1876-77	Ⓤ
1877-78	Ⓐ
1878-79	Ⓑ
1879-80	Ⓒ
1880-81	Ⓓ
1881-82	Ⓔ
1882-83	Ⓕ

NORWICH

- There were at least a dozen silversmiths active in Norwich as early as the 13thC.

- Norwich was granted power of assay in 1423.

- The original mark showed a castle surmounting a lion passant, and wares were also stamped with the date letter and maker's mark.

- In the first part of the 17thC, a mark depicting a crowned seeded rose was introduced, to be replaced in the last half of the century by a stemmed rose.

- Assaying of silver in Norwich was sporadic and probably ceased altogether after 1701.

Date	Mark	Date	Mark	Date	Mark
1624-25	A	1632-33	I	1641-42	S
1625-26	B	1633-34	K	1642-43	T
1626-27	C	1634-35	L	1643-44	V
1627-28	D	1635-36	M	*From 1645-87 a variety of marks were used*	
1628-29	E	1636-37	N		
1629-30	F	1637-38	O		
1630-31	G	1638-39	P		
1631-32	H	1639-40	Q		
		1640-41	R		

Date	Letter
1688	a
1689	b
1690	C
1691	D
1692	E
1693	F
1694	G
1695	H
1696	I
1697	K

SILVER

YORK

- York was granted power of assay in 1423, but there is evidence of the existence of a local touch from as early as 1410.
- The original mark was a half leopard's head with a fleur-de-lys joined together in one shield, followed by date letters and makers' marks.
- The leopard's head was replaced by a half-seeded rose by the end of the 17thC, and in 1701 it was changed to five lions passant on a cross.

Date	Mark	Date	Mark
1642-43	m	1661-62	G
1643-44	n	1662-63	H
1644-45	O	1663-64	J
1645-46	p	1664-65	K
1646-47	q	1665-66	L
1647-48	r	1666-67	M
1648-49	ſ	1667-68	N
1649-50	t	1668-69	O
1650-51	U	1669-70	P
1651-52	w	1670-71	Q
1652-53	X	1671-72	R
1653-54	y	1672-73	S
1654-55	Z	1673-74	T
1655-56	A	1674-75	V
1656-57	B	1675-76	W
1657-58	C	1676-77	X
1658-59	D	1677-78	Y
1659-60	E	1678-79	Z
1660-61	F	1679-80	A

Date	Mark	Date	Mark	Date	Mark
		1618-19	M	1630-31	Z
1607-08	A	1619-20	N	1631-32	a
1608-09	B	1620-21	O	1632-33	b
1609-10	C	1621-22	P	1633-34	c
1610-11	D	1622-23	Q	1634-35	d
1611-12	E	1623-24	R	1635-36	e
1612-13	F	1624-25	S	1636-37	f
1613-14	G	1625-26	T	1637-38	g
1614-15	H	1626-27	U	1638-39	h
1615-16	I	1627-28	W	1639-40	i
1616-17	K	1628-29	X	1640-41	k
1617-18	L	1629-30	Y	1641-42	l

Date	Mark	Date	Mark	Date	Mark	Date	Mark	Date	Mark
	(mark)		(marks)	1777-78	B	1797-98	L	1819-20	h
1680-81	B	1701-02	A	1778-79	C	1798-99	M	1820-21	i
1681-82	C	1702-03	B	1779-80	D	1799-1800	N	1821-24	k
1682-83	D	1703-04	C	1780-81	E	1800-01	O	1824-25	n
1683-84	E	1704-05	D	1781-82	F	1801-02	P	1825-26	o
1684-85	F	1705-06	–	1782-83	G	1802-03	Q	1826-27	p
1685-86	G	1706-07	F	1783-84	H	1803-04	R	1827-28	q
1686-87	H	1707-08	G	1784-86	J	1804-05	S	1828-29	r
1687-88	I	1708-09	–		(marks)	1805-06	T	1829-30	s
1688-89	K	1709-10	(I)	1787-88	A	1806-07	U	1830-31	t (mark)
1689-90	L	1710-11	–	1788-89	B	1807-08	V	1831-32	u
1690-91	M	1711-12	–	1789-90	C	1808-09	W	1832-33	v
1691-92	N	1712-13	m	1790-91	d	1809-10	X	1833-34	w
1692-93	O	1713-14	–	1791-92	e	1810-11	Y	1834-35	x
1693-94	P	1714-15	O	1792-93	f	1811-12	Z	1835-36	z
1694-95	Q	In c1716, the practice of assaying silver was discontinued. It resumed c1776.		1793-94	g	1812-15	a		(marks)
1695-96	R			1794-95	h	1815-17	b	1836-37	A
1696-97	S		(marks)	1795-96	i	1817-18	c	1837-38	B
		1776-77	A	1796-97	k	1818-19	d	1838-39	C

35

SILVER

1839-40	D	1844-45	I	1849-50	O	1853-54	S	1858-59	X
1840-41	E	1845-46	K	1850-51	P *Leopard's head not used after 1850*	1854-55	T		
1841-42	F	1846-47	L	1855-56	U				
1842-43	G	1847-48	M	1851-52	Q	1856-57	V		
1843-44	H	1848-49	N	1852-53	R	1857-58	W		

NEWCASTLE

- Newcastle was granted power of assay in 1423.

- The original mark was three separate castles in a shield.

- Marking was erratic until 1702 when the figure of Britannia and the lion's head erased, denoting the new standard, were introduced.

- In 1720, when the old standard was restored, the leopard's head and lion passant replaced the old mark, used with the town mark and date letter.

- After 1728, the lion passant faces to the right.

- The last assay of silver at Newcastle was in April 1884.

1716-17	Ⓐ		*Between 1721–28 shapes of shields and lion passant vary; the lion may face left*	
1717-18	Ⓟ			
1718-19	Ⓑ	1728-29	𝔅	
1719-20	Ⓓ	1729-30	𝔜	
1720-21	Ⓒ	1730-31	𝔎	
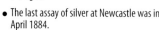		1731-32	𝔏	
1721-22	𝔞	1732-33	𝔐	
1722-23	𝔟	1733-34	𝔑	
1723-24	𝔠	1734-35	𝔒	
1724-25	𝔡	1735-36	𝔭	
1725-26	𝔢	1736-37	𝔮	
1726-27	𝔣	1737-38	𝔎	
1727-28	𝔤	1738-39	𝔰	

		1704-05	Ⓒⓛ	1707-11	𝔉
1702-03	𝔄	1705-06	Ⓓ	1711-12	𝔊
1703-04	𝔅	1706-07	𝔈	1712-16	𝔥

SILVER

Year	Mark	Year	Mark	Year	Mark	Year	Mark	Year	Mark
	[town marks]	1757-59	S	1785-86	T	1803-04	N	1822-23	H
1739-40	T	1759-60	[script a]	1804-05	[symbol marks]	1823-24	O	1823-24	I
1740-41	A	1760-69	[symbol]	1786-87	U	1805-06	P	1824-25	K
1741-42	B	1769-70	[symbol]	1787-88	W	1806-07	Q	1825-26	L
1742-43	C	1770-71	[symbol]	1788-89	X	1807-08	R	1826-27	M
1743-44	D	1771-72	[symbol]	1789-90	Y	1808-09	S	1827-28	N
1744-45	E	1772-73	[symbol]	1790-91	Z	1809-10	T	1828-29	O
1745-46	F	1773-74	G	1791-92	A	1810-11	U		[symbol marks]
1746-47	G	1774-75	H	1792-93	B	1811-12	W	1829-30	P
1747-48	H	1775-76	I	1793-94	C	1812-13	X	1830-31	Q
1748-49	J	1776-77	K	1794-95	D	1813-14	Y	1831-32	R
1749-50	K	1777-78	L	1795-96	E	1814-15	Z	1832-33	S
1750-51	L	1778-79	M	1796-97	F	1815-16	A	1833-34	T
1751-52	M	1779-80	N	1797-98	G	1816-17	B	1834-35	U
1752-53	N	1780-81	O	1798-99	H	1817-18	C	1835-36	W
1753-54	O	1781-82	P	1799-1800	I	1818-19	D	1836-37	X
1754-55	P	1782-83	Q	1800-01	K	1819-20	E	1837-38	Y
1755-56	Q	1783-84	R	1801-02	L	1820-21	F	1838-39	Z
1756-57	R	1784-85	S [symbol]	1802-03	M	1821-22	G		

SILVER

	🖼 🖼 🖼 🖼	1857-58	Ⓢ	1876-77	ⓝ
1839-40	Ⓐ	1858-59	Ⓣ	1877-78	ⓞ
1840-41	Ⓑ	1859-60	Ⓤ	1878-79	ⓟ
1841-42	Ⓒ 🖼	1860-61	Ⓦ	1879-80	ⓠ
1842-43	Ⓓ	1861-62	Ⓧ	1880-81	ⓡ
1843-44	Ⓔ	1862-63	Ⓨ	1881-82	Ⓢ
1844-45	Ⓕ	1863-64	Ⓩ	1882-83	ⓣ
1845-46	Ⓖ	1864-65	ⓐ	1883-84	ⓤ
1846-47	Ⓗ	1865-66	ⓑ		
1847-48	Ⓘ	1866-67	ⓒ		
1848-49	Ⓙ	1867-68	ⓓ		
1849-50	Ⓚ	1868-69	ⓔ		
1850-51	Ⓛ	1869-70	ⓕ		
1851-52	Ⓜ	1870-71	ⓖ		
1852-53	Ⓝ	1871-72	ⓗ		
1853-54	Ⓞ	1872-73	ⓘ		
1854-55	Ⓟ	1873-74	ⓚ		
1855-56	Ⓠ	1874-75	ⓛ		
1856-57	Ⓡ	1875-76	ⓜ		

GLASGOW

- Glasgow had its own corporation of hammermen by 1536, and in 1681 they adopted a date letter system.

- This became obsolete in the early 18thC, when the letters S (Sterling, or Scottish), O and E were frequently used, together with the town mark showing a tree with a bird in its upper branches, a bell suspended from a lower branch and a fish laid at the base.

- Silver marked with the early Glasgow hallmark is rarely seen.

- In 1819, the lion rampant of Scotland and the sovereign's head were added, and in 1914 the thistle standard mark was used.

- The Glasgow office closed in 1964.

Year	Mark	Year	Mark	Year	Mark
		1704-05	ỳ	1830-31	L
		1705-06	ȝ	1831-32	M
		1706-07	A	1832-33	N
		1707-08	B	1833-34	O
		1709-10	D	1834-35	P
		Between 1710–1819 S Z E F O were found		1835-36	Q
				1836-37	R
		(town marks)		1837-38	S
		1819-20	A	1838-39	T
		1820-21	B	1839-40	U
		1821-22	C	1840-41	V
		1822-23	D	1841-42	W (marks)
1688-89	(town mark)	1823-24	E	1842-43	X
1681-82	a	1824-25	F	1843-44	Y
1682-83	b	1825-26	G	1844-45	Z
1683-84	c	1826-27	H	(marks)	
1684-85	d	1827-28	I	1845-46	A
1685-86	e	1828-29	J	1846-47	B
1686-87	f	1829-30	K	1847-48	C
1687-88	g				
1689-90	h				
1690-91	i				
1691-92	k				
1692-93	l				
1693-94	m				
1694-95	n				
1695-96	o				
1696-97	p				
1697-98	q				
1698-99	r				
1699-1700	s				
1700-01	t				
1701-02	u				
1702-03	w				
1703-04	x				

SILVER

Year	Mark	Year	Mark	Year	Mark	Year	Mark	Year	Mark
1848-49	🛡🦁🐟	1866-67		1885-86	O	1904-05	R	1922-23	Z
1849-50		1867-68		1886-87	P	1905-06		1923-24	a
1850-51		1868-69		1887-88	Q	1906-07		1924-25	b
1851-52		1869-70		1888-89	R	1907-08	K	1925-26	c
1852-53		1870-71	Z	1889-90	S	1908-09	L	1926-27	d
1853-54		1871-72	A	1890-91	T	1909-10	M	1927-28	e
1854-55		1872-73	B	1891-92	U	1910-11	N	1928-29	f
1855-56		1873-74	C	1892-93	V	1911-12	O	1929-30	g
1856-57		1874-75	D	1893-94	W	1912-13	P	1930-31	h
1857-58		1875-76	E	1894-95	X	1913-14	Q	1931-32	i
1858-59		1876-77	F	1895-96	Y	1914-15	🛡🦁👑	1932-33	j
1859-60		1877-78	G	1896-97	Z	1915-16	R	1933-34	k
1860-61		1878-79	H	1897-98	A	1916-17	S	1934-35	l
1861-62		1879-80	I	1898-99	B	1917-18	T	1935-36	m
1862-63		1880-81	J	1899-1900	C	1918-19	U	1936-37	n
1863-64		1881-82	K	1900-01	D	1919-20	V	1937-38	o
1864-65		1882-83	L	1901-02	E	1920-21	W	1938-39	p
1865-66		1883-84	M	1902-03	F	1921-22	X	1939-40	q
		1884-85	N	1903-04	G		Y	1940-41	r

Date	Mark	Date	Mark
		1959-60	
1941-42	S	1960-61	N
1942-43	t	1961-62	O
1943-44	u	1962-63	P
1944-45	v	1963-64	R
1945-46	W		
1946-47	X		
1947-48	Y		
1948-49	Z		
1949-50	A		
1950-51	B		
1951-52	C		
1952-53	D		
1953-54	e		
1954-55	F		
1955-56	G		
1956-57	H		
1957-58	I		
1958-59	J		

CHESTER

- There are records in town deeds of silversmiths working in Chester as early as the 13thC.

- Marking of silver was not regulated until the end of the 17thC, even though there was a guild of goldsmiths who supervised the manufacture, assay and sale of plate from the early 15thC.

- Chester's town mark showed a shield bearing the arms of the city. The accompanying marks were similar to those of London of the same period, with the lion passant, leopard's head and date letter.

- The office stopped operating on 24 August 1962.

Date	Mark	Date	Mark
		1718-19	S
1701-02	A	1719-20	T
1702-03	B		
1703-04	C	1720-21	U
1704-05	D	1721-22	V
1705-06	E	1722-23	W
1706-07	F	1723-24	X
1707-08	G	1724-25	Y
1708-09	H	1725-26	Z
1709-10	I		
1710-11	K		
1711-12	L		
1712-13	M		
1713-14	N		
1714-15	O		
1715-16	P		
1716-17	Q		
1717-18	R		

SILVER

Year	Mark	Year	Mark	Year	Mark	Year	Mark	Year	Mark
	🦁 ⚜ 🛡	1744-45	T	1763-64	n	1781-82	f	1800-01	D
1726-27	A	1745-46	U	1764-65	O	1782-83	g	1801-02	E
1727-28	B	1746-47	V	1765-66	P	1783-84	h	1802-03	F
1728-29	C	1747-48	W	1766-67	Q	1784-85	i	1803-04	G
1729-30	D	1748-49	X	1767-68	R	1785-86	k	1804-05	H
1730-31	E	1749-50	Y V	1768-69	S	1786-87	l ?	1805-06	I
1731-32	F	1750-51	Z	1769-70	T	1787-88	m	1806-07	K
1732-33	G	1751-52	a	1770-71	T	1788-89	n	1807-08	L
1733-34	H	1752-53	b	1771-72	U	1789-90	O	1808-09	M
1734-35	I	1753-54	c	1772-73	V	1790-91	p	1809-10	N
1735-36	K	1754-55	d	1773-74	W	1791-92	q	1810-11	O
1736-37	L	1755-56	e	1774-75	X	1792-93	r	1811-12	P
1737-38	M	1756-57	f	1775-76	Y	1793-94	S	1812-13	Q
1738-39	N	1757-58	G	1776-77	a	1794-95	t	1813-14	R
1739-40	O	1758-59	h	1777-78	b	1795-96	u	1814-15	S
1740-41	P	1759-60	i		🦁 ⚜ 🛡	1796-97	V	1815-16	T
1741-42	Q	1760-61	k	1778-79	C	1797-98	A	1816-17	U
1742-43	R	1761-62	l	1779-80	d	1798-99	B	1817-18	V
1743-44	S	1762-63	m	1780-81	e	1799-1800	C	1818-19	A 🦁

SILVER

Year	Mark	Year	Mark	Year	Mark	Year	Mark	Year	Mark
(town marks)		1837-38	T	1855-56	R	1874-75	l	1892-93	I
1819-20	B	1838-39	U	1856-57	S	1875-76	m	1893-94	K
1820-21	C	(town marks)		1857-58	T	1876-77	n	1894-95	L
1821-22	D	1839-40	A	1858-59	U	1877-78	o	1895-96	M
1822-23	D	1840-41	B	1859-60	V	1878-79	p	1896-97	N
1823-24	E	1841-42	C	1860-61	W	1879-80	q	1897-98	O
1824-25	F	1842-43	D	1861-62	X	1880-81	r	1898-99	P
1825-26	G	1843-44	E	1862-63	Y	1881-82	s	1899-1900	Q
1826-27	H	1844-45	F	1863-64	Z	1882-83	t	1900-01	R
1827-28	I	1845-46	G	1864-65	a	1883-84	u	1901-02	A
1828-29	K	1846-47	h	1865-66	b	1884-85	A	1902-03	B
1829-30	L	1847-48	I	1866-67	c	1885-86	B	1903-04	C
1830-31	M	1848-49	K	1867-68	d	1886-87	C	1904-05	D
1831-32	N	1849-50	L	1868-69	e	1887-88	D	1905-06	E
1832-33	O	1850-51	M	1869-70	f	1888-89	E	1906-07	F
1833-34	P	1851-52	N	1870-71	g	1889-90	F	1907-08	G
1834-35	Q	1852-53	O	1871-72	h	(town marks)		1908-09	H
1835-36	R	1853-54	P	1872-73	i	1890-91	G	1909-10	I
1836-37	S	1854-55	Q	1873-74	k	1891-92	H	1910-11	K

43

SILVER

Year	Mark	Year	Mark	Year	Mark
	🛡️ 🛡️	1929-30	P	1948-49	X
1911-12	L	1930-31	Q	1949-50	Y
1912-13	M	1931-32	ff	1950-51	Z
1913-14	N	1932-33	G	1951-52	A
1914-15	O	1933-34	B	1952-53	B
1915-16	P	1934-35	H	1953-54	C
1916-17	Q	1935-36	K	1954-55	D
1917-18	R	1936-37	L	1955-56	E
1918-19	S	1937-38	W	1956-57	F
1919-20	T	1938-39	A	1957-58	G
1920-21	U	1939-40	O	1958-59	H
1921-22	V	1940-41	P	1959-60	J
1922-23	W	1941-42	Q	1960-61	K
1923-24	X	1942-43	R	1961-62	L
1924-25	Y	1943-44	S	1962	M
1925-26	Z	1944-45	T		
1926-27	a	1945-46	U		
1927-28	b	1946-47	V		
1928-29	c	1947-48	W		

Barnstaple

Goldsmiths worked in Barnstaple as early as 1370 and are recorded until the end of the 17thC. The earliest mark used from 1272 until c1624 was adapted from the borough mark, which showed a bird in a circular stamp. It later changed to a triple-turreted tower derived from the city's arms and was used until the end of the 17thC.

Bristol

The city was appointed an assay office in 1701 but there are no traces of an assay office or of a guild of goldsmiths. Some marks have been found with the Bristol arms (a ship issuing from a castle) included, but their origin is not yet confirmed.

Carlisle

Marks dating from the 16thC and 17thC, showing a single four-petalled rose, have been identified as the marks of the city of Carlisle. A similar rose appears in the arms of the city.

Dundee

The silversmiths of Dundee were incorporated with other trades as 'hammermen'. Although it is known that smiths were working earlier, the oldest record books date from 1587. The arms of the burgh of Dundee, which were used as a town mark, are 'azure a pot of growing lilies argent'. The pot has two handles although they vary in form. The flowers also vary, in number and style. Early in the 19thC a thistle was added.

Hull

Early pieces made in Hull are marked with the letter H as the town mark; this was replaced in the 17thC by the town arms showing three ducal coronets. It is unlikely that there was an assay office here, but its distance from London and other towns made the registering of its own marks practical.

King's Lynn

The town arms of King's Lynn were adapted to make the town mark. This shows three dragons' heads with crosses in their mouths on a shield background. Marks have been recorded from here from c1632.

SILVER

Leeds

Leeds goldsmiths adopted the arms of the town, showing a golden fleece, for its town mark. The mark is usually found on wares dating from the 17thC.

Leicester

Silversmiths were active from the early 16thC until the 17thC. The only mark that may be ascribed is the wyvern mark.

Lewes

Lewes smiths marked their wares with a chequered shield derived from the town seal. Spoons bearing this mark survive from the late 16thC and early 17thC.

Lincoln

The city was granted power of assay in 1423, although silversmiths are known to have worked in Lincoln from the 12thC onwards. The town mark was derived from the city arms and depicted a fleur-de-lys. The mark is most commonly found on spoons.

Perth

Goldsmiths are recorded in Perth from the 12thC. The goldsmiths became part of the Hammermen's Incorporation from 1431. The old name for Perth was St. John'stoun and its device was the earliest mark used on Perth silver- a 'lamb bearing the banner of St. Andrew'. From the late 18thC an 'eagle displayed' was used.

Plymouth

Plymouth marks date from c1600 to c1700. The town mark was adapted from the city arms and depicted a saltire between four castles. From the early 18thC the goldsmiths used the Exeter Assay Office to register marks.

Poole

Marks depicting a scallop shell, dating from the 16thC and 17thC, have been identified as the coat-of-arms of Poole. Three similar shells appear in the town arms.

Salisbury

The city was granted power of assay in 1423. However, there are few marks found that can be definitely associated with the city. One mark used by more than one goldsmith is the 'pig', probably copying the lion passant of London.

Sherborne

Although there is no known town mark, there are records of one famous local goldsmith, Richard Orenge, who used marks 1572–1607 depicting his initials and a pellet, surrounded by two circles of pellets.

Southampton

The marks depicted have been found on church plate in the Southampton area and roses are used in the arms of Southampton. The rose cannot be exclusively attributed to Southampton; it was also used as a maker's mark in London, Newcastle and Norwich.

Taunton

Evidence of goldsmiths using the town mark of a 'T' and a tun can be found on apostle spoons and a paten, dating between 1665 and 1689.

Truro

A mark showing the initials TR surrounded by a circle of pellets found on Cornish spoons of the 17thC is thought to be the town mark of Truro.

BRITISH & IRISH MAKERS

- Listed below is a selection of some of the best-known British and Irish silversmiths from the 17thC to the early 20thC.

- London was by far the most popular centre for British silversmiths. Therefore, unless otherwise stated, assume all the following makers were London-based.

- Before a silversmith could register a mark on his own, he served as an apprentice to a 'Master' (a qualified silversmith). After a specified time, the apprentice was granted his freedom (that is, he was no longer apprenticed) and was permitted to set up business on his own.

- Many silversmiths went on to become members of the Company of Gold & Silversmiths, a process known as 'liveried'. Some then progressed to become part of the governing body, becoming members of court, then wardens. The head of the company was known as the Prime Warden.

- Gold and silversmiths (also known as plateworkers) can be divided into two categories: largeworkers and smallworkers. Largeworkers made objects of a more substantial size such as baskets, dishes, tureens and large hollow wares. Smallworkers made small pieces such as vinaigrettes, wine labels and matchboxes.

 William Abdy
Registered marks as a smallworker in 1763, 1767, 1769, 1779 and 1784. Died 1790.

 Robert Abercromby
Registered marks in 1731, 1739 and 1740.

 Stephen Adams & William Jury
Registered marks c1758 and 1759.

 Charles Aldridge
Registered mark in partnership with Henry Green in 1775 and further marks in 1786 and 1789.

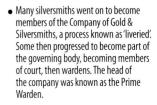 **Edward Aldridge**
Registered marks in 1724 and 1739. Registered mark in partnership with John Stampe in 1753.

 William Alexander
Apprenticed to Isabella Archer in 1707 and made a freeman in 1716. Registered mark in 1743.

 Joseph Allen & Mordecai Fox
Allen registered his first mark in partnership with Fox in 1730 from St Swithin's Lane, and his second with him in 1739.

John Angell
Son of John Angell Snr. and apprenticed to him in 1825. John Angell Snr. did not register a mark but worked with his brother Joseph. John Angell Jnr. registered a mark in partnership with uncle, Joseph Angell, in 1831.

 Joseph Angell
Apprenticed to Henry Nutting in 1796. Registered two marks in 1811 and 1824.

 George Angell & John Charles Angell
John Charles Angell went into business with his eldest son, George Angell. Registered marks in 1840 and 1844. After his father's death in 1850, George continued the business under the name George Angell & Co. until 1860, when further marks were registered. He died in 1884.

 Peter Archambo Snr.
Apprenticed to Jacob Margas. Registered marks in 1721, 1722 and 1739. Prolific output.

 Peter Archambo Jnr. & Peter Meure
Peter Archambo Jnr. was a cousin of Peter Meure. Registered mark in 1750.

 Charles Robert Ashbee
(1863–1942) An influential designer of early 20thC silver, Ashbee trained as an architect before becoming a leader of the Arts and Craft movement. He was a founder member of the Guild of Handicraft, which consisted of a circle of artist-craftsmen who sought to perpetuate medieval hand-craftsmanship. He had no formal training as a silversmith but his early work was especially innovative.

 Asprey & Co. Ltd.
(c1781–) The company is believed to have been founded in 1781 in Mitcham, Surrey by William Asprey. By 1805, the firm had moved to London premises and was under the direction of Francis Kennedy. Early in the 19thC Kennedy was joined by Charles Asprey Snr. who, by the middle of the century, had left Kennedy and set up his own premises in New Bond Street. Throughout the 19thC and afterwards Asprey was acclaimed as one of London's leading silver manufacturers and retailers.

SILVER

William Atkinson
Apprenticed to William Bellasis of the Merchant Taylors' Company in 1718, becoming a freeman in 1725. Registered two marks as a largeworker that year.

William Bagnall
Apprenticed to Gabriel Sleath in 1736. Registered mark as a largeworker in 1744.

Thomas Bamford
Apprenticed to Charles Adam in 1703. Registered first two marks as a largeworker in 1720 and another in 1739. Known as a caster maker as was his master and his apprentice, Samuel Wood.

John Barbe
Registered marks as largeworker in 1735, 1739 and 1742.

Edward, John & William Barnard
One of the oldest surviving firms. William served apprenticeship under his father, Edward in 1815. They registered a mark together with William's brother, John, in 1829. Known as Edward Barnard & Sons from 1829–1910, and Barnard & Sons Ltd. from 1910 to the present day.

Edward Barnard, Edward Barnard Jnr., John Barnard & William Barnard
Registered their mark together in 1829 as plateworkers.

George Baskerville
Apprenticed to Joseph Sanders in c1732. Registered marks in 1738, 1745, 1751, 1755 (in partnership with William Sampel) and 1780.

Hester Bateman
(1709–94) Hester Needham married John Bateman, a maker of gold watch chains, in 1732, and established a family silversmith business. Early pieces were mainly flatwares but they later graduated to larger domestic objects and produced vast quantities of silverwares. Hester Bateman first registered her own mark in 1761, a year after her husband's death. However, her mark is rarely found on pieces dated earlier than 1774 because during the intervening years she was occupied running the shop and co-ordinating commissions. After 1774, she appears to have concentrated on her own silversmithing, producing refined shapes with restrained decoration, often restricted to beading along the

edges. Much of Hester Bateman's work was commissioned by other contemporary silversmiths, many of whom obliterated her mark and replaced it with their own. On her retirement in 1790, Bateman handed over the business to her sons, Peter and Jonathan. On Jonathan's death in 1791, his widow Ann registered a mark in conjunction with her brother-in-law. Her son, William, joined the partnership in 1800 and the three registered a joint mark. The mark of Peter and William Bateman was registered on Ann's retirement in 1805. Peter remained in control of the business until 1839, when he handed it down to his nephew, William.

Peter & Jonathan Bateman

Peter and Jonathan were sons of Hester Bateman. Peter and Jonathan registered a mark in 1790, followed by a further six marks in 1791.

Peter & Ann Bateman

Ann married Jonathan Bateman in 1769 and on his death joined in partnership with brother-in-law Peter, registering a mark with him in 1791.

Peter, Ann & William Bateman

Ann registered mark with brother-in-law Peter (see above) and her son William (see below) in 1800.

Peter & William Bateman

Son and grandson of Hester Bateman (see above), registered mark in 1805. (See also below.)

William Bateman

Born 1774, second son of Jonathan and Ann Bateman, grandson of Hester. Registered marks with Peter and Ann Bateman in 1800, with Peter only in 1805, and alone in 1815. Sold the family business c1840.

Samuel Bates

Registered marks in 1728 and 1744. Liveried in 1752.

Richard Bayley

Apprenticed to Charles Overing from 1699, and to John Gibbons in 1704. Became a freeman in 1706. Registered marks in 1708, 1720 and 1739. Liveried in 1712. His son Richard Bayley was apprenticed to Samuel Spindler.

Richard Beale

Apprenticed to Jonathan Newton in 1722 and John Le Sage in 1725. Registered three marks in 1733, 1739 and 1746.

William Bell
Apprenticed to William Burton in 1748. Registered marks in 1759, 1763, 1769, 1772, 1774 and 1777.

Edward Bennett
Apprenticed to Henry Miller in 1720 and Samuel Hutton in 1725. Registered marks in 1727, 1731, 1737, 1739 and 1747. Liveried in 1737.

John Berthellot
Registered marks in 1738, 1739, 1746 and 1750.

Cornelius Bland
Served apprenticeship under James Bishop, registered marks in 1772 and 1788. Thomas Young served as his apprentice in 1779.

James & Elizabeth Bland
Elizabeth was the widow of Cornelius. Registered mark in partnership with her son James in 1794.

George Boothby
Registered marks in 1720 and 1739.

Matthew Boulton
Important Birmingham-based manufacturer. Formed partnership with John Fothergill 1762–82. Boulton was active in establishing the Birmingham Assay Office.

Prior to 1773, when the Birmingham office opened, his silver was marked with Chester mark. Boulton died in 1809 but his manufactory continued throughout the 19thC.

Thomas Bradbury & Sons
Sheffield plate manufacturers run by Thomas Bradbury and sons from 1831. Registered marks in 1860, 1906 and 1907.

Bennett Bradshaw & Co.
Apprenticed to Paul de Lamerie (see page 65) in 1721. Registered marks in 1737 and 1739 in partnership with Robert Tyrill.

John Bridge
Apprenticed to William Rogers of Bath; became partner to Philip Rundell (see page 71) in 1788. By 1797, Bridge and Rundell were Goldsmiths and Jewellers to the King. Bridge registered two marks in 1823, one with a crown. Joined Court in 1831; became Prime Warden in 1839. Died 1849.

Walter Brind
Apprenticed to John Raynes in 1736 and to his brother, Henry Brind, in 1742. Became a freeman in 1743. Registered marks in 1749, 1751, 1757 and 1781. Liveried in 1758.

Alice & George Burrows
Alice was probably the widow of George. Registered marks in partnership with son George in 1801, 1804, 1810 and 1818. Died c1819.

 William Burwash
Registered mark in partnership with Richard Sibley (see page 72) in 1805. Other marks registered alone in 1812 and 1813.

 John Cafe/Case
(active 1740–57) Registered mark with Goldsmiths in 1742 and specialized in the manufacture of candlesticks, chambersticks, snuffers and trays. His business went bankrupt in 1757. It was taken over subsequently by his brother William.

 William Cafe/Case
Brother of John Cafe, apprenticed to him in 1742 and to Simon Jouet in 1746. Cafe was a prolific maker of cast candlesticks. Registered mark in 1757.

 Isaac Callard
A spoonmaker who registered New Standard and sterling marks as a largeworker in 1726. Subsequently registered marks in 1739, 1747 and 1750.

 Paul Callard
Son of Isaac and Marguerite Callard, born 1724. Registered marks in 1752 and 1759.

 Edward Capper
Registered marks as a smallworker in 1792 and 1813.

 Carrington & Co.
The company was first listed as John Carrington in 1873, becoming Carrington & Co. c1880. The company still active. Registered marks from 1895 to 1907.

 John Carter
Registered two marks in 1776. He is known to have bought candlesticks made and marked in Sheffield, which he overstruck with his own mark.

 Benjamin Cartwright
Goldsmith who registered marks in 1732, 1739, 1748 and 1757. Cartwright Snr. had a son, Benjamin Jnr., who was also a silversmith.

 Henry Chawner
Born 1764, only son of Thomas Chawner (see page 54). Registered marks in 1786, 1787, and in partnership with John Emes, 1796. Liveried in 1791. Died 1851.

SILVER

Mary Chawner
Widow of William Chawner. Registered mark as a spoon maker in 1834 and registered a further five marks in 1835.

Thomas Chawner
Apprenticed to Ebenezer Coker. Registered several marks in 1773, 1775 and 1783. Liveried in 1771. Worked with brother William from c1759.

Charles Chesterman
Apprenticed to George Greenhill Jones. Registered marks in 1741, 1752 and 1771. Son Charles was apprenticed to him.

Ebenezer Coker
Apprenticed to Joseph Smith in 1728. Registered marks in 1738, 1739, 1745, 1751 and some time after 1758. Also registered a mark in partnership with Thomas Hammond c1759.

William Comyns & Sons
William Comyns established the company c1859. Registered first mark in 1859. Sons, Charles and Richard Harling Comyns, joined the firm c1885. William died in 1916 and Charles in 1925. Richard formed a limited company in 1930. Richard died in 1953 when the firm was bought

by Bernard Copping; it survives today. Registered marks as William Comyns & Sons. Last mark registered in 1905.

Edward Cooke
Apprenticed to Charles Jones in 1713. Registered mark in 1735. Liveried in 1737 and joined the Court of Assistants in 1755.

Augustine Courtauld
A prolific Huguenot maker of domestic pieces. Apprenticed to Simon Pantin, became a freeman in 1708. Courtauld married Anne Bardin in 1709. Registered marks in 1708, 1729 and 1739. Best-known work is the State Salt of the City of London of 1730. Other works include large two-handled trophies, salvers and tableware items produced as presentation gifts for notable families, including the Russian Royal family.

Samuel Courtauld
Son of Augustine Courtauld, Samuel was born in 1720. He was apprenticed to his father in 1734, took over the business on his father's retirement in 1746. Registered marks in 1746 and 1751. Married Louisa Perina Ogier in 1749. Liveried in 1763.

Louisa Perina Courtauld
Daughter of French silk weaver Peter Ogier of Poitou, Louisa Perina Ogier married silversmith Samuel Courtauld in 1749. She took over the family business on her husband's death in 1765. She formed a partnership with George Cowles. Unregistered marks date from c1765 and c1768; registered mark dates from 1777. Louisa died in 1807.

Louisa & Samuel Courtauld
Born 1752, Samuel was son of Louisa and Samuel Courtauld. Mother and son partnership registered mark in 1777. In 1780, the business was taken over by John Henderson. Samuel emigrated to America and died there in 1821.

Louisa Courtauld & George Cowles
George Cowles was apprenticed to Louisa and her husband, Samuel. Registered a mark in partnership with Louisa c1768. Cowles registered a separate mark in 1777. Died 1811.

Robert Albin Cox
Apprenticed to Humphrey Payne in 1745 and to John Payne in 1750. He was freed in 1752. Registered marks in 1752, 1758 and 1759. Liveried in 1791; elected to Court in 1813.

Sebastian & James Crespell
Huguenot makers, Sebastian and James were probably brothers who may have served apprenticeships with Edward Wakelin (see page 75). Names appear as suppliers of Wakelin's firm in 1769. Four sons were apprenticed to the trade – André, Sebastian, Honoré and James.

Paul Crespin
Much acclaimed Huguenot silversmith. Crespin was apprenticed to Jean Pons. First marks date from c1720. Registered marks in 1739, 1740 and 1757.

Creswick & Co.
Sheffield-based manufacturers. As T, J & N Creswick, registered first mark in 1810. Business was founded by Thomas and James, and Nathaniel joined in 1819. In 1855 the firm became Creswick & Co.

William Cripps
Apprenticed to David Willaume Jnr. in 1731; became a freeman in 1738. Registered marks in 1743, 1746 and 1751. Liveried in 1750.

SILVER

 John Crouch Jnr.
Son of goldsmith, John Crouch Snr., to whom he was apprenticed. Registered mark in 1799 as partner with Thomas Hannam (see page 62) and alone in 1808. Liveried in 1829. Died in 1837.

 Francis Crump
Apprenticed to Gabriel Sleath in 1726; became a freeman in 1741. Registered marks in 1741, 1745, 1751, 1753 (in partnership with Gabriel Sleath) and 1756.

 Thomas & Jabez Daniell
Father and son partnership that dated from c1771. Thomas registered a mark on his own in 1774.

 Thomas Daniell & John Wall
Registered mark in 1781. Partnership had dissolved by 1782 when Daniell registered another separate mark.

 William Darker
Apprenticed to Richard Bayley. Registered marks in 1719, 1720, 1724 and 1731. Liveried in 1725.

 Isaac Davenport
Registered mark in 1697, from Gutter Lane. Registered two further marks c1697.

 Samuel Davenport
Registered marks in 1786 and, in partnership with Edward Davenport, in 1794. Had a son of the same name who was apprenticed to William Seaman in 1809.

 Abraham de Oliveyra
May have trained as a goldsmith and engraver in Holland. Registered marks c1725 and 1739.

 James Dixon & Sons
Based in Sheffield. Started c1806 by James Willis Dixon; registered marks in 1912 and 1914. James registered marks alone in 1873 and 1910.

 J W Dobson
Henry Holmes Dobson and John Wilkinson Dobson founded the business, which became Dobson & Sons when Henry was joined by his two sons Thomas William and Henry Holmes Jnr. Thomas William and Henry Holmes registered mark in 1877. Thomas William registered marks in his own name for the firm in 1886, 1895 and 1898.

 Jane Dorrell & Richard May
Jane Dorrell was the widow of William (also a silversmith). She registered marks with Richard May (her apprentice) in 1766, 1769 and 1771.

Christopher Dresser

(1834–1904) An important English designer and writer who was preoccupied with the need for good design and the importance of mechanization. He designed revolutionary modern-style silverwares and electroplate for the firms of Elkington (see page 58) and Hukin & Heath from 1875 to 1878. Most of his designs are extremely simple and geometric in appearance; exposed rivets are a favourite motif.

Louis Dupont

Huguenot silversmith and son of Pierre du Pont, a goldsmith from Poitiers. Registered a mark in 1736 and 1739.

Elizabeth Eaton

Inherited a firm c1845 on death of husband, William. In 1858 her son John joined the firm, which became known as Elizabeth Eaton & Son. Registered marks in 1845, 1847, 1864 and 1858.

William Eaton

Registered marks in 1813, 1824, 1828, 1830, 1834, 1836, 1837 and 1840.

James Charles Edington

Registered marks in 1828, 1837, 1845, 1854 and 1856.

Edward Edwards

Son of John Edwards. Edward was apprenticed to John Mewburn. Registered a mark in 1811, and two in 1816. His son, of the same name and also a silversmith, registered marks in 1828, 1840 and 1841.

John Edwards

Apprenticed to Thomas Prichard. Registered marks in partnership with George Pitches in 1723. Further marks registered in 1724, 1739 and 1753.

William Edwards

Son of Edward Edwards. Apprenticed to his father as an engraver. Registered marks in 1800, 1809 and 1823. Liveried in 1846 and died in 1860.

William Eley Snr.

Apprenticed to William Fearn. Registered mark when in partnership with George Pierrepont in 1777. Other marks registered in 1778, 1790 and 1795; registered marks in 1797 and 1802 in partnership with William Fearn, and in 1808 with William Chawner and Fearn; final mark without Chawner was registered 1814. Eley was liveried in 1806 and died in 1824.

SILVER

William Eley Jnr. & William Fearn

William Eley Jnr. was son of William Eley Snr. (see page 57) and was apprenticed to his father. Registered marks with William Fearn in 1824, 1825 and 1826.

Elkington & Co.

(1801–65) Company renowned for the development of the electroplate process, which revolutionised the production of inexpensive silverware. The technique was first patented by the company in 1840. Later, Elkington granted special licences to other companies, such as the French firm Christofle, to produce their own electroplate.

 William Elliott

Apprenticed to Richard Gardner. Registered mark in partnership with J W Storey in 1809 and alone in 1813.

John Emes

Apprenticed to William Woollett. Registered mark in partnership with Henry Chawner (see page 53) in 1796 and further marks alone in 1798 and 1802. Business taken over by his wife Rebecca and brother William.

Rebecca Emes & Edward Barnard

Supplied wares to Rundell, Bridge & Rundell (see page 71). Rebecca was the widow of John Emes. She took over his business in partnership with William Emes, she registered marks with Edward Barnard (see page 50) in 1808, 1818, 1821 and 1825.

Thomas England

Goldsmith; apprenticed to John Martin Stocker in 1714 and to Samuel Margas in 1716. Became a freeman in 1728. Registered two marks, one sterling and one New Standard, date from 1725. Registered marks in 1816, 1820 and 1823.

Thomas Eustace

Prominent West Country silversmith, apprenticed to Richard Jenkins. Registered mark in 1779. Member of the Exeter Goldsmiths' Company in 1774 and Warden between 1777 and 1779.

Edward Feline

Apprenticed to Augustine Courtauld in 1709. Registered marks in 1720 and 1739. Liveried in 1731.

 **Fenton Brothers Ltd.**
Specialist cutlers and sword makers from Sheffield. Business was established by John Frederick Fenton and Frank Fenton c1875. Frank, Samuel and Alfred John Fenton registered marks separately between 1883 and 1888. Firm became Fenton Brothers Ltd. in 1896.

 Edward Fernell
Apprenticed to William Grundy in 1762. A registered mark in partnership with Grundy dates from 1779 (see page 62). Fernell registered marks alone in 1780, 1781 and 1787.

Andrew Fogelberg
(1732–93) Came from Sweden and was probably already trained when he arrived in London c1770. He formed a partnership with Stephen Gilbert, working with him from 1780 to 1793. Fogelberg seems to have pioneered the application of decorative cameo-like medallions to his silverwares. Paul Storr (see page 74) was apprenticed to Fogelberg.

 Andrew Fogelberg & Stephen Gilbert
Registered mark in partnership in 1780. Stephen Gilbert was apprenticed to Edward Wakelin (see page 75) and worked in the Wakelin establishment.

 John Fossey
Apprenticed to Thomas Tearle in 1724; became a freeman in 1731. Registered marks in 1733, 1734 and 1739.

  John Fountain
Brother of William Fountain. Apprenticed to Robert Grace Cleets and Daniel Smith. Registered marks in 1792, 1793 (in partnership with John Beadnell) and alone in 1797.

William Fountain
Younger brother of John Fountain. Registered mark in partnership with Daniel Pontifex in 1791. Partnership dissolved by 1794, when William Fountain registered a mark alone.

   Charles Fox Jnr.
Son of Charles Fox Snr. Registered marks in 1822, 1823 and 1838. Different marks used for various types of ware; the number of marks registered reflect the popularity of Fox's products.

George Fox
Probably the son of George Fox of Rundell, Bridge & Rundell. Partner with Charles Thomas Fox from c1838 when the latter inherited his grandfather's silver works.

 Charles Thomas Fox & George Fox
Silver works established in 1801 by James Turner and Charles Fox Snr. Grandson, Charles Thomas Fox registered marks in 1841 and 1843.

 William Frisbee
Registered mark with John Edwards (see page 57) in 1791, alone in 1792 and with Paul Storr (see page 74) in 1792.

 John Frost
Apprenticed to Gawen Nash in 1750 and to Thomas Gladwin in 1757. Registered marks in 1757.

 Crispin Fuller
Registered marks in 1792, 1796 and 1823. Son Jeremiah apprenticed to James Shallis in 1813.

 Phillip Garden
Goldsmith and jeweller. Apprenticed to Gawen Nash in 1730. Registered marks in 1738, 1739, 1744, 1748 and 1751. Liveried in 1746; resigned in 1763.

 Robert Garrard
In 1792, Robert Garrard joined the partnership established by George Wickes (see page 76) and Edward Wakelin (see page 75), which became known as Wakelin & Garrard. John Wakelin (see page 76) passed the business to Garrard when he retired in 1802. Garrard was succeeded by sons Robert (1793–1881), James (1795–1870) and Sebastian (1798–1870) when he died in 1818. The company remained in the Garrard family's hands and became the Crown Jewellers and Goldsmiths in 1830.

 William Garrard
Apprenticed to Samuel Laundy in 1729, to Jeffrey Griffith in 1732 and to Ralph Maiden. Registered marks in 1735, 1739 and 1749.

 George Giles
Smallworker. Registered mark in 1762 and one in partnership with John Cooper in 1765.

 George Gillingham
Apprenticed to Anthony Nelme in 1692. Marks registered in 1703, 1718 and 1721.

 Thomas Gilpin
Served apprenticeship with John Wells in 1720. Registered marks in 1730 and 1739.

Samuel Godbehere

Plateworker. Registered marks in 1784, 1786 in partnership with Edward Wigan; 1789, 1792, 1800 in partnership with Edward Wigan and James Bult, as Samuel Godbehere & Company; and in 1818 in partnership with James Bult. Godbehere probably had connections with the City of Bath as he was given power of attorney for the signing of the entry into the register of two Bath goldsmiths, William Bottle and James Burden.

Philip Goddard

Apprenticed to Peter White in 1711. Became a freeman in 1720. Registered marks in 1725 and 1738.

Benjamin Godfrey

Registered marks in 1732 and 1739.

Eliza Godfrey

(active 1741) The most prolific of the women silversmiths operating in the mid 18thC. Godfrey had been briefly married to silversmith Abraham Buteaux, and married Benjamin Godfrey in 1732. However, in 1741 she was left widowed. Between her marriages and after her second husband's death she registered her own marks, continuing the business with enormous success and producing such fine silverwares that she has been referred to as 'the best woman silversmith of the 18thC'.

Benjamin Godwin

Apprenticed to Joseph Clare in 1722 and William Darker in 1727. Registered mark in 1730.

Richard Gosling

Apprenticed to Matthew Cuthbert in 1712. Registered marks in 1733, 1739 and 1748. Business continued with sons Richard and Joseph.

James Gould

Brother of William Gould. Apprenticed to David Green in 1714. Registered marks in 1722, c1733, 1739 and 1743.

William Gould

Apprenticed to his brother James Gould in 1724. Registered marks in 1732, 1734, 1739, 1748 and 1753.

Henry Greene

Apprenticed to Thomas Allen in 1693. Registered marks in 1700 and 1720. Liveried in 1708.

SILVER

 William Grundy
Apprenticed to Edward Vincent in 1731. Registered marks alone in 1743, 1748 and 1777, and in 1779 in partnership with Edward Fernell.

 William Grundy & Edward Fernell
Fernell (see page 59) was apprenticed to Grundy in 1762. In 1779, they registered a mark in partnership. Fernell registered a mark on his own in 1780, possibly after Grundy's death.

 Richard Gurney & Co.
Apprenticed to Richard Bayley in 1717. Became a freeman in 1724. Registered his first mark in partnership with Thomas Cook in 1727. Trading as Richard Gurney & Co. the company registered marks in 1734, 1739, 1749 and 1750. Richard's younger brother John was apprenticed to him in 1730.

 William Gwillim & Peter Castle
Gwillim was apprenticed to John Gamon in 1731. Peter Castle was apprenticed to Thomas Ruch in 1734 and became a freeman c1741. They registered a mark in partnership in 1744.

 Martin, Hall & Co. of Sheffield
Prominent Sheffield manufacturer founded in 1854 by Ebenezer Hall and Robert Martin.

 William Hall
Apprenticed to Jonathan Bateman in 1787 and to Ann Bateman in 1791. Registered mark in 1795.

 Henry Hallsworth
Apprenticed to William Cafe in 1762. Recorded mark c1769.

 Messrs Hancock & Co.
Charles Frederick Hancock worked with Storr and Mortimer until 1843 when he founded his own business. Hancock & Co. is still in business as a retailer.

 Thomas Hannam & John Crouch Snr.
(active c1773). Thomas Hannam had previously formed partnership with Richard Mills with whom he registered a mark in 1765.

 Harrison Bros. & Howson
Sheffield-based company, run by James William Harrison, Henry Harrison and William Howson. Founded in 1866. The partners registered marks separately: James in 1896, Henry in 1880 and William in 1866.

John Harvey

Served apprenticeship under Matthew Judkins; became a freeman in 1737. Registered marks in 1738, 1739, 1745, 1746, 1748 and 1750.

Charles Hatfield

Served apprenticeship under Joseph Barbutt and David Williams. Registered marks in 1727 and 1739. Died c1740 and his mother or widow Susannah Hatfield registered a mark.

Hawksworth, Eyre & Co.

Sheffield and London-based manufacturers. Charles Hawksworth and John Eyre set up the firm in 1852. Registered marks in 1862, 1900 and 1912.

Thomas Heming

Son of a Midlands merchant. Served apprenticeship under Peter Archambo. Registered marks in 1745 and c1767. Liveried in 1763. Appointed Principal Goldsmith to King George III in 1760. From this date a crown appeared above his mark until 1782, when he was ousted from the position after an investigation into his apparently excessive charges. He was replaced by Jeffreys & Jones.

David Hennell

The first of a silver-making dynasty. Apprenticed to Edward Wood in 1728, freeman in 1735. Married Hannah Broomhead in 1736. Registered marks in 1736, 1763 (in partnership with his son) and 1768. In 1737 he took as apprentice his half-brother William, but the latter never registered a mark. Son Robert was apprenticed to him in 1756. Liveried in 1763 and retired from business in 1773 to become Deputy Warden. Gave evidence on marking procedure at the assay office to the Parliamentary Committee. Died 1785.

Robert Hennell

Born in 1741, son of David Hennell to whom he was apprenticed in 1756. Registered marks in partnership with father in 1763 and 1768, and alone in 1772 and 1773. By 1795, registered mark in partnership with son, David; mark of 1802 was registered with David and a second son, Samuel. Worked until his death in 1811, when his son Samuel took over with the registration of his own mark in 1812.

SILVER

 Robert, David & Samuel Hennell
David was the son of Robert Hennell and brother of Samuel. Apprenticed to father in 1782. Father and sons registered two marks in 1802.

 Robert & Samuel Hennell
Samuel was Robert's son and registered a mark in partnership with his father and brother David in 1802. Samuel and Robert registered a mark without David in 1802.

 Henry Herbert
Became Subordinate Goldsmith to the King from 1736 to 1740. Registered marks in 1734, 1735, 1739 and 1748.

 George Hindmarsh
Registered mark in partnership with Robert Abercromby (see page 48) in 1731 and alone in 1731, c1736, 1739 and 1753.

 Samuel Hitchcock
Apprenticed to John Brace in 1699. Registered marks in 1713, 1720 and 1730. Liveried in 1721 and resigned in 1743.

 William Holmes & Nicholas Dumée
Registered mark in partnership in 1773. Holmes registered marks alone in 1776 and 1792. J S Denwall and his son John Gwyn Holmes served as his apprentices.

 John Hopkins
Served as an apprentice under Andrew Archer in 1716 and became a freeman in 1723. Registered two marks, both undated c1720–24.

 Charles Hougham
Apprenticed to Henry Corry in 1764. Registered marks in 1769, 1773, 1779, 1785 and 1786.

 Solomon Howland
Apprenticed to Thomas Whipham in 1752 and to Edward Day in 1759. Became a freeman in 1760. Registered two marks in 1760.

 John S Hunt
A partner in Mortimer & Hunt from 1839 to 1844. Company became Hunt & Roskill when Mortimer retired in 1843. Hunt registered marks in 1839, 1844 and 1855. Registered marks as Hunt & Roskill Ltd. in 1897, 1901 and 1912.

 Samuel Hutton
Apprenticed to Edward Jennings in 1717; became a freeman in 1724. Registered marks in 1724, 1725, 1734 and 1740.

Charles Frederick Kandler

Registered marks in partnership with James Murray in 1727; registered marks on his own, one undated and others in 1739 and 1768.

Jeremiah King
Apprenticed to William Scarlett, became a freeman in 1722. Registered marks in 1723, 1736, 1739, 1743 and 1744.

Archibald Knox
(1854–1933) Born and educated on the Isle of Man. His observation of the Celtic remains there is reflected in the Celtic motifs decorating his silverwares. He made silver and other metalwares for Liberty & Co. and was the most important of their designers. He was commissioned by Liberty to produce designs for the Cymric silverware range.

Henry Lake
John Elliott Lake & Son was established in 1833 by Henry Lake in Exeter. From 1874 the firm continued under direction of son John Elliot, who was joined by his son John Henry. John Elliott Lake and John Henry Lake registered a mark in 1903.

Edward Lambe

Son of George Lambe. Apprenticed to mother Jane Lambe in 1731. Registered marks in 1740 and 1742. Lambe had two sons, George and John, who were also silversmiths.

John Lambe
Son of Edward Lambe. John registered marks in 1774, 1780, 1782, 1783, 1785, 1788, 1790 and 1791.

Paul de Lamerie
(1688–1751) A Huguenot, born in the Low Countries. His parents brought him to England in 1689, after the Revocation of the Edict of Nantes. He served his apprenticeship with Pierre Platel in 1703 and registered his first mark in 1712. De Lamerie worked consistently in Britannia silver until 1732, even though after 1720 it was no longer compulsory. He registered a sterling silver mark in 1732. In 1739, de Lamerie registered a third mark and moved his workshop to Gerrard Street in London where he died in 1751. Although other 18thC silversmiths equalled de Lamerie in skill, his work is undoubtedly the most popular and collectable today.

Samuel Laundy
Possibly of Huguenot origin. Apprenticed to James Goodwin in 1720. Registered marks in 1727, 1731 (in partnership with Jeffrey Griffith) and alone in 1732.

Abraham Le Francis
Registered marks c1742 and in 1746.

John Hugh Le Sage
A Huguenot, father of Augustin and Simon. Apprenticed to Lewis Curey in 1708. Registered marks in 1718, 1722 and 1739. Liveried in 1740; became Subordinate Goldsmith to the King under George II.

Simon Le Sage
Son of goldsmith John Hugh Le Sage. Apprenticed to father in 1742 and later to Peter Meure. Registered marks in 1754. Also became Subordinate Goldsmith to the King from c1754–59.

John & Henry Lias
Father and son registered marks in 1818 and 1819.

John Lingard
Apprenticed to William Fawdery in 1709. Registered marks in 1718, 1719 and 1720.

Seth Lofthouse
Apprenticed to William Wakefield in 1676. Registered mark in c1699. Active until c1722.

Matthew Lofthouse
Apprenticed to George Hanson of the Wax Chandlers' Company in 1689, freeman in 1697. Registered marks in 1705 and 1721.

William Looker
Apprenticed to Benjamin Bentley in 1706; became a freeman in 1713. Registered marks in 1713 and 1720.

Edward Lowe
Registered marks in 1760, 1769, 1770, 1771 and 1777.

John Ludlow
Apprenticed to George Cox in 1706; became a freeman in 1713. Registered marks in 1713 and 1720.

Robert Makepeace & Richard Carter
Registered mark together in 1777. In 1778, Richard Carter registered a new mark.

Thomas Mann
Apprenticed to William Juson in 1706 and to Henry Clark. Registered marks in 1713, 1720, 1729, 1736 and 1739.

British & Irish Makers

 James Manners
Registered marks in 1726, 1734
and 1739. His son James Manners
Jnr. was also a silversmith,
registering a mark in 1744.

 Mappin & Webb
Prominent English engravers,
silversmiths and cutlers, still
thriving today. Company founded
by Joseph Mappin in Sheffield
in 1810. Taken over by sons as
Mappin Brothers, who later joined
with a brother-in-law to become
Mappin & Webb. Began producing
good-quality electroplate
silverware in the mid 19thC; now
concerned mainly with jewellery.
Earlier marks were registered by
John Newton Webb and George
Webb, plateworkers, in 1866 and
1880. As Mappin & Webb Limited
they registered marks in 1899
and 1900.

 Nathaniel Mills
Prolific Birmingham-based
manufacturer of snuff boxes,
vinaigrettes, wine labels and other
small wares. Registered marks in
1803 and 1825–55.

 Thomas Moore
Apprenticed to George Greenhill
Jones in 1743. Registered mark
in 1750.

 Anthony Nelme
Registered mark in 1697.
Elected Assistant to the Court of
Goldsmiths in 1703 and made
Warden in 1717 and 1722.

 Francis Nelme
Son of Anthony Nelme and
apprenticed to him in 1712.
Registered marks in 1723 and
1739.

 Hannah Northcote
Born in 1761, wife of Thomas
Northcote. Hannah registered first
mark after her husband's death in
1798 and another in 1799. Died
in 1831.

 Thomas Northcote
Registered marks in 1776, 1777,
1779, 1782, 1784. Registered a
mark with George Bourne in 1794.

 Henry Nutting
Apprenticed to Charles Wright
in 1782 and Thomas Chawner in
1784. Registered mark in 1796.
Registered mark with Robert
Hennell (see page 63).

 Francis Pages
Apprenticed to David Williams in
1718. Registered marks in 1729
and 1739. Liveried 1737.

Richard Pargeter

Apprenticed to Andrew Archer in 1718 and to James Wilkes in 1724; became a freeman in 1726. Registered marks in 1730, 1737 and 1739. Liveried in 1737.

John Parker & Edward Wakelin

Registered mark c1758. The partnership continued until 1777 when Edward Wakelin took William Taylor as his partner.

Thomas Parr

Son of Thomas Parr (also a silversmith). Registered marks in 1733 and 1739. Liveried in 1750; joined Court in 1735 and was a Warden from 1771 to 1773.

A & F Parsons

(of Edward Tessier) Arthur Martin Parsons and Frank Herbert Parsons continued the business of Edward Tessier (or Vander & Hedges, as it was also called). Registered marks in 1910 and 1911. The company became Tessiers Ltd. in 1920, with the Parsons as first directors. It continues today.

Humphrey Payne

Apprenticed to Roger Grange in 1694; became a freeman in 1701. Registered marks in 1701, 1720 and 1739. Liveried in 1708;

became a member of Court in 1734 and was made a Warden from 1747 to 1749.

John Payne

Son of Humphrey Payne; apprenticed to him in 1733. Registered mark in 1751. Liveried in 1740.

Edmund Pearce

Apprenticed to Henry Beesley in 1693 and to Phillip Rollos in 1697. Registered marks in 1705 and 1720.

Wiliam & Robert Peaston

In partnership from 1756 until 1763. Registered mark in 1756.

Abraham Peterson

Registered first mark in partnership with Peter Podio in 1783, and second alone in 1792.

S J Phillips

Well-known retail business of silversmiths and jewellers founded in 1869 by Solomon Joel. Firm continued by son, Edmund A Phillips. Registered mark in 1901.

Thomas Phipps & Edward Robinson

Thomas was son of James Phipps and apprenticed to him in 1769. Phipps and Robinson registered marks in 1783 and 1789. They were later joined by James Phipps

(Thomas's son). Father and son registered a mark in 1816.

Pezé Pilleau
The son of Pezé Pilleau Snr. Apprenticed to John Charter in 1710. Registered two marks, undated, between 1720 and 1724 and a third in 1739.

William Pitts
Son of Thomas Phillip; apprenticed to him in 1769. Registered marks in 1781, 1786, 1791 and 1806.

William Pitts & Joseph Preedy
William Pitts registered mark in partnership with Preedy in 1791. Partnership dissolved by 1799, when Pitts registered mark on his own.

Pierre Platel
(active 1699–1719) Was a French Huguenot silversmith who became a member of the Goldsmiths' Company in 1699. Platel had several apprentices who became successful in their own right, the most celebrated was Paul de Lamerie (see page 65).

William Plummer
Apprenticed to Edward Aldridge in c1746; registered marks in 1755, 1774 and 1789.

Thomas Boulton Pratt & Arthur Humphreys
Partners registered mark in 1780. Pratt's son, Thomas, was apprenticed to him in 1785. Two other sons were also silversmiths and served apprenticeship under him.

Joseph Preedy
Apprenticed to Thomas Whipham in 1765 and, in 1766, to William Plummer. Registered first marks alone in 1777, second mark in partnership with William Pitts in 1791 and third mark alone in 1800.

William & James Priest
William and James Priest were probably brothers. James Priest was apprenticed to William in 1750. Registered mark in c1764. They are recorded working together until 1773.

Benjamin Pyne
Apprenticed to George Bowers in 1667. Registered mark in 1696, further mark registered undated. He was Subordinate Goldsmith to the King for the coronation of George I in 1714.

SILVER

 John Quantock
Apprenticed to James Gould in 1726. Registered marks after 1739 and in 1754.

 Philip Rainaud
Huguenot maker, apprenticed to Pierre Platel in 1700. Registered marks in 1708 and 1720. Liveried in 1721.

 Omar Ramsden & Alwyn Carr
Registered a joint mark in 1898. They were among the new generation of silversmiths who carried on the ideals of traditional hand-crafted techniques into the modern age of mass production. Ramsden (1873–1939) registered a Gothic-style mark when he set up on his own in 1918. He often applied a Latin signature in addition to his mark.

 Charles Rawlings & William Summers
Registered mark in partnership in 1829 and a further six new marks in 1840.

 Charles Reily & George Storer
Registered marks in 1829 and in 1840.

 Roberts & Belk
Sheffield company established in c1809 as Furniss, Pole & Turner. Samuel Roberts and Charles Belk formed partnership in 1885. Samuel retired in 1879 and was succeeded by Charles. The firm became a limited company in 1901. Registerd marks as Samuel Roberts & Charles Belk in 1865 and 1878. Registered marks as Roberts & Belk Ltd. in 1906 and 1938.

 Thomas Robins
Apprenticed to cousin John Robins in 1786. Registered mark in 1801. Liveried in 1811; died in 1859.

 Philip Roker
Apprenticed to Joseph Barbutt in 1707. Registered marks in 1720 and 1739. Sons Matthew and John and wife Elizabeth also silversmiths.

 Emick Romer
(Emmich Römer) Norwegian working in London from c1758 to 1795. Son of an Oslo goldsmith, registered mark c1758.

 Gundry Roode
Apprenticed to Alexander Roode. Registered marks in 1710, 1721 and 1737.

Richard Rugg
Apprenticed to James Gould in 1738. Registered marks in 1754 and 1775. Son Richard was apprenticed to him in 1763. Liveried in 1772; died c1795.

Rundell, Bridge & Rundell
(1788–1842) Established by Philip Rundell (1743–1827), became one of London's most successful makers. In 1788, Rundell formed a partnership with John Bridge (see page 52) and they were joined by Edmund Waller Rundell in 1803. In 1806, the company was recorded as employing 1,000 workers. Many of its more important wares were made by specially commissioned independent silversmiths, such as Paul Storr (see page 74) and Benjamin Smith (see page 73). John Flaxman modelled figures for some of the enormous presentation pieces in which the company specialized.

 Philip Rundell
Partner in one of the leading silver manufacturers of the late 18thC and early 19thC. Rundell was apprenticed to William Rogers, jeweller, of Bath, and arrived in London c1768. He worked for Theed and Pickett, made a partner with Pickett in 1772 and became sole owner between 1785 and 1786. Rundell took John Bridge (see page 52) as partner in 1788 and nephew Edmund Waller Rundell as partner in 1803, and the company became Rundell, Bridge & Rundell. Registered marks in 1819 and 1822. Appointed Goldsmith and Jeweller to the King in 1797. Rundell retired from his business c1823 and, at that time, John Bridge registered his own mark.

 Joseph Sanders
Apprenticed to Thomas Eweds in 1714, and Joseph Belcher in 1719. Registered marks in 1730 and 1739. Liveried c1727.

 Adey, Joseph & Albert Savory
Albert was the son of Adey and brother of Joseph. Registered marks together in 1833 and 1834. Registered further marks by Albert and Joseph only in 1735, as A B Savory & Sons.

 Richard Scarlett
Son of William Scarlett (see page 72); apprenticed to him in 1710. Registered marks in 1720 and 1723.

SILVER

William Scarlett
Apprenticed to Simon Scott in 1687. Registered marks c1697, 1720, 1722 and 1725.

John Schofield
Also 'Scofield'. Registered mark in 1776 in partnership with Robert Jones and further marks alone in 1778 and 1787. Worked for the retailers and Royal Goldsmiths Jeffreys, Jones & Gilbert.

William Schofield
Apprenticed to George Grace in 1786. Registered marks in 1820 and 1833.

John Schuppe
Probably of Dutch origin. Registered mark in 1753.

Digby Scott & Benjamin Smith
Originally working in Birmingham, later Greenwich, Scott and Smith also worked with Matthew Boulton (see page 52). Scott and Smith (see page 73) registered a mark in partnership in 1802 and 1803. In 1807, Smith registered a mark alone.

William Shaw
Apprenticed to Edward Holliday in 1715. Registered marks in 1729, 1739 and 1745.

Richard Sibley
Son of John Sibley of Bath; apprenticed to Daniel Smith and in 1791 to Robert Sharp. Registered mark with Thomas Ellerton in 1803, alone in 1805, with William Burwash (see page 53) in 1805 and alone in 1812. Liveried in 1811. Had various apprentices, including son Richard in 1821.

William Simons
Apprenticed to Richard Hawkins in 1757 and to Robert Salmon. Registered two marks in 1776. In 1776 George Whittingham was apprenticed to him.

James Slater
Apprenticed to John Ford in 1718, and to Thomas Kidder and John Allbright. Registered mark c1725.

Gabriel Sleath
Apprenticed to Thomas Cooper in 1691. Registered marks in 1707, 1720, 1739 and 1753. Liveried in 1712.

William Robert Smiley
Registered marks in 1842 and 1844, and more as a spoon maker until final one in 1857.

Benjamin Smith
(b.1764) One of the major suppliers of wares to Rundell, Bridge & Rundell (see page 71). Many designs

were very similar to those of Paul Storr (see page 74). Before 1792, he formed a company known as Boulton & Smith with his brother, James, and Matthew Boulton (see page 52) of Birmingham. In 1801, a disagreement led to the formation of a new partnership between Boulton and James Smith. In 1802, Benjamin moved to Greenwich. He formed a partnership with Digby Scott (see page 72), registering marks in 1802 and 1803. In 1807, Smith registered a mark alone. In partnership with brother James, he registered a mark in 1809. Further marks were registered in 1812, 1814, 1816 (with his son Benjamin Jnr.) and in 1818.

Daniel Smith & Robert Sharp

Registered mark in c1763. Registered mark with a new partner, Richard Carter in 1778, and without Carter in 1780.

James Smith

Apprenticed to Peter White in 1710; became a freeman in 1718. Registered marks in 1718 and 1720.

George Smith

Registered marks in 1774, 1775, 1776, 1778, 1780 and 1782. Registered mark in partnership with William Fearn in 1786.

George Smith & Thomas Hayter

Hayter was apprenticed to George Smith in 1782. Registered mark in partnership with Smith's son George in 1792.

Nathaniel Smith & Co.

Prominent Sheffield silversmith. Registered mark in 1780.

William Smith Snr.

Apprenticed to his father Samuel Smith in 1742; freedom 1749. Registered marks in 1758, 1763, 1764, 1769 and 1774. Died c1781.

William Soame

Apprenticed to Samuel Hitchcock in 1713. Registered two marks in 1723; further marks date from 1732 and 1739.

Francis Spilsbury Snr.

Apprenticed to Richard Green in 1708. Registered marks in 1729 and 1739. Liveried in 1737.

Francis Spilsbury Jnr.

Son of Francis Spilsbury. Registered mark in 1767. Liveried in 1763.

Nicholas Sprimont

Important Huguenot maker, born in Liège in 1716. Registered first mark in 1743. In 1748 he became a full-time porcelain manufacturer. Died in 1754.

Ambrose Stevenson

Apprenticed to father Thomas Stevenson in 1692. Registered marks in 1707 and 1720.

Paul Storr

(1771–1844) Originally apprenticed to the Swedish-born plate worker, Andrew Fogelberg (see page 59). He opened his own shop in 1796. Between 1807 and 1819 he worked in association with Rundell, Bridge & Rundell (see page 71). In 1822, Storr formed a partnership with John Mortimer that was to last until 1838.

William Sumner

Apprenticed to Thomas Chawner in 1763. Registered marks in 1775 (in partnership with Richard Crossley), alone in 1776, 1777, 1780, 1782, 1784, and various further marks before his last in 1803. Mary Sumner, his wife, registered a mark in 1807 when William had probably died.

John Swift

Registered marks c1728, 1739, and two in 1757. Son John apprenticed to him in 1750.

David Tanqueray

Registered marks in 1713 and 1720.

Ann Tanqueray

Widow of David Tanqueray. Registered two marks on the death of her husband c1725. She was probably not a goldsmith herself as wares bearing her mark were clearly made by journeymen she employed.

John Tayler

Apprenticed to Henry Green in 1714. Registered marks in 1728 and 1734.

Joseph Hayes Taylor

Birmingham-based silversmith. Registered mark in 1880; went out of business in 1888.

Samuel Taylor

Apprenticed to John Newton in 1737. Registered marks in 1744 and 1757.

Thomas Tearle

Apprenticed to Gabriel Sleath in 1707. Registered marks in 1720 and 1739.

Thomas & Co.

Bond Street retail silversmiths established by John William Thomas in 1759. Francis Bourne Thomas took control c1871 and the name changed to F B Thomas & Co. Francis registered first marks in 1874. Registered further marks in 1875 and 1887. In 1900 John

William Thomas and C H Townly took over and continued the business until c1941 when an air raid demolished it.

James Tookey
Registered marks in 1750 and 1762; liveried in 1758. Married Elizabeth Tookey. Son Thomas Tookey served as apprentice in 1766.

Thomas Tookey
Son of James Tookey, apprenticed to him in 1766. Registered marks in 1773, 1775, 1779 and 1780.

John Tuite
Apprenticed in 1703 to John Matthews of Dublin. Tuite worked in Dublin between 1710 and 1720, where he used a similar mark to the one he later registered in London. Tuite moved to London in 1723 and registered an undated mark c1724 and another in 1739.

Walter Tweedie
Registered marks in 1775, 1779 and 1781.

George Unite
Unite & Sons were established in Birmingham in 1825 by George Unite. In 1852 they were listed in London as silversmiths. Registered marks date from 1886 and 1889.

Aymé Videau
Important Huguenot silversmith. Apprenticed to David Willaume in 1723. Registered marks date from 1739; an earlier mark is probably missing from the register. Liveried in 1746.

Edward Wakelin
Partner in important firm of silversmiths, apprenticed to John Le Sage in 1730. By 1747 he had joined George Wickes and registered first mark in 1747 (very similar to that of Wickes). Wakelin took over the business and appointed a new partner, John Parker (see page 68), c1758. From 1761 the business became Parker & Wakelin Partnership, with Parker as senior partner. Wakelin continued in business until 1777 when his son John (see page 76) and William Taylor joined the firm.

John Wakelin
Son of Edward Wakelin (see page 75), apprenticed to him in 1766. He became a freeman in 1779. Registered marks with William Taylor in 1776 and 1777; registered mark in partnership with Robert Garrard (see page 60) in 1792.

James Wakely & Frank Clarke Wheeler
Worked for Henry John Lias & Son. Registered marks in 1896 and 1906.

 Walker & Hall
Sheffield-based gold and silver workers founded in 1843, initially specializing in electroplate. Sir John Bingham, Hall's nephew, joined and ran the company until his death in 1916, when he was succeeded by Sir Albert Bingham. They registered marks as gold and silver workers in 1903, 1906, 1907 and 1913. In 1971, they became part of Mappin & Webb (see page 67), and later British Silverware Ltd.

 Thomas Wallis
Apprenticed to Thomas Wallis Snr. Registered marks in 1778, 1780–89, 1792 and 1810 (the last was in partnership with Jonathan Hayne).

 Benjamin Watts
Apprenticed to Walter Bradley in 1691. Registered marks in 1698 and 1720.

 Samuel Welder
Apprenticed to Robert Keble in 1707 and became a freeman in 1714. Registered marks 1714, 1717, 1720 and 1729.

 Benjamin West
Apprenticed to James Smith in 1725 and became a freeman in 1733. Registered marks in 1738 and 1739.

 Thomas Whipham
Apprenticed to Thomas Farren in 1728. Registered marks in 1737, 1739 (in partnership with William Williams), 1740 and 1757 (in partnership with Charles Wright (see page 77). Liveried in 1746.

 Fuller White & John Fray
Registered mark in 1745. Partnership had dissolved by 1748 when Fray registered a separate mark.

   George Wickes
(1698–1761) Was apprenticed to Simon Wastell on 2 December 1712 and registered marks in 1722.

Christopher & Thomas Wilkes Barker
Thomas was the son of Christopher and apprenticed to William Fearn in 1787. Registered marks in partnership in 1800 and 1804; partnership dissolved by 1805 when Thomas registered a mark alone.

Denis Wilks
Registered marks in 1737, 1739, 1747 and in 1753 in partnership with John Fray. The partnership had dissolved in 1756, when Fray registered his own mark.

James Wilks
Registered marks in 1722, c1728, 1739 and 1742.

David Willaume Snr.
Huguenot silversmith. Registered marks c1697, 1719 and 1720. Daughter Ann married David Tanqueray (see page 74).

David Willaume Jnr.
Apprenticed to his father, David. Registered marks in 1728 and 1739.

Samuel Wintle
Registered mark in 1778 in partnership with Thomas Wintle. Registered marks alone in 1779, 1783 and 1792.

Edward Wood
Apprenticed to James Roode in 1715; became a freeman in 1722. Registered marks in 1722, 1735 and 1740. David Hennell served as his apprentice in 1728.

Samuel Wood
Apprenticed to Thomas Bamford in 1721; became a freeman in 1730. Registered marks in 1733, c1737, 1739, 1754 and 1756.

William Woodward
Apprenticed to William Pearson in 1719 and to George Wickes in 1722; became a freeman in 1726. Registered marks in 1731 and 1743.

Charles Wright
Apprenticed to Thomas Whipham in 1747; became a freeman in 1754. Registered mark in partnership with Whipham (see page 76) in 1757. Registered further marks alone in 1775 and 1780. Liveried in 1758; became a member of Court in 1777 and a Warden from 1783 to 1785. Died in 1815.

Richard Zouch
Apprenticed in 1720 to Francis Plymley and to William Darker in 1735; became a freeman in 1737. Registered marks in 1735 and 1739.

SILVER

AMERICAN & CANADIAN HALLMARKING

- American makers marked their wares with their name or initials (see pages 79–82) but there was no uniform regulation of silver purity, nor any comprehensive system of date or town marking.

- Although American marks are scant, cities such as New York and Boston had official societies, similar to the system of guilds that presided over European silversmiths; occasionally the place of origin is marked in full alongside the maker's mark.

- Modern silver produced in the USA should be marked with the maker's name and numbers indicating the purity. The word STERLING appears on silver of .925 purity.

- From 1700 to 1763, when Canada was under French rule, marks were similar to those used in France. Makers used their initials with a fleur-de-lys, a crown or a star.

- The word 'MONTREAL' or 'QUEBEC' was sometimes marked on pieces made there. H or HX or XNS may be marked on pieces made in Halifax, Nova Scotia and ST J or NB for St John, New Brunswick.

Imitations of English marks

Late 18thC

CANADIAN DATE LETTERS

1898	a	1903	d	1929	O	1934	g	1939	D
1899	b	1925	k	1930	P	1935	j	1940	E
1900	C	1926	l	1931	q	1936	A	1941	F
1901	d	1927	m	1932	r	1937	B	1942	G
1902	e	1928	n	1933	I	1938	C	1943	H

AMERICAN & CANADIAN MAKERS

- Listed below is a selection of some of the best-known American and Canadian silversmiths and retailers. Where precise birth or death dates are unknown the dates indicate the years in which the maker is believed to have been active.

- There was no American equivalent to the English hallmarking system, although some American-made pieces may bear State marks.

- Most American silver is marked with a maker's or retailer's mark. Many makers used their whole name within a border.

Joseph Anthony Jnr.
Philadelphia, PA, 1762–1814.
Josiah Austin
Charlestown or Boston, MA, c1760–70.
Ball, Black & Co.
New York, NY, c1850–75.
Ball, Tompkins & Black
New York, NY, c1840–50.
Conrad Bard
Philadelphia, PA, c1825–50.
Samuel Bartlett
Concord or Boston, MA, 1750–1821.
 Henry Birks & Sons
Montreal, Canada, founded by Henry Birks 1879. In 1893 he formed a partnership with his sons William, John and Gerald. It was bought by a subsidiary of Gorham Company in 1907.
 Carence Crafters
Chicago, IL, 1908–c1918

Samuel Casey
South Kingston, RI, c1753–55.
F H Clark & Co.
Memphis, TN, c1850–55.
John Coburn
Boston, MA, 1725–1803.
Jeremiah Dummer
(1645–1718) Credited with being the first American-born silversmith. Served his apprenticeship with John Hull in Boston, and later engraved plates for Connecticut's first paper money.
Stephen Emery
Boston, MA, 1725–1801.
Charles Fans
Annapolis, MD, c1785–1800.
Hyram Fans
Annapolis, MD, c1790–1800.
William Fans Jnr.
Annapolis, MD, Norfolk, VA, Havana, Cuba, Edenton, NC, 1782–1803.

John W Forbes
New York, NY, 1810–40.

William Forbes
New York, NY, c1775–1830.

Daniel C Fueter
New York, NY, c1755–1805.

William Gale & Son
New York, NY, c1825–50.

Baldwin Gardiner
Philadelphia, PA, New York, NY,
c1815–40.

Gelston & Treadwell
New York, NY, c1835–38.

William Gilbert
New York, NY, c1775–1818.

Gorham Manufacturing Co.
(1818–) Company founded by
Jabez Gorham (1792–1869) in
Providence, RI. In 1868, T J
Pairpoint joined the company and
products were marked with both a
date and trade mark.

Hayden, Gregg & Co.
Charleston, SC, c1845–52.

Grosjean & Woodward
Boston, MA, 1847–50, New York,
NY, 1850s.

Newell Harding
Haverhill and Boston, MA,
1796–1862.

John Hastier
New York, NY, d.1791.

William Haverstick
Lancaster and Philadelphia, PA,
c1780–98.

Heintz Art Metal Co.
Buffalo, NY, 1906–30.

Daniel Henchman
Boston, MA, 1730–75.

**William B Heyer
& Jesse Gale**
New York, NY, c1800–07.

William Hollingshead
Philadelphia, PA, c1755–85.

William Holmes
Boston, MA, 1742–1825.

A Jacobi
Baltimore, MD, c1878–80.

Robert Jarvie
(1865–1941) Jarvie Shop,
Chicago, IL, c1905–c1920

Jones, Ball & Co.
Boston, MA, c1850–52.

Kalo Shop
Chicago, IL, 1900–70.

Robert Keyworth
Washington DC, c1830–33.

Samuel Kirk & Sons
Baltimore, MD, 1845–60.

Mary C Knight
Worked for Handicraft Shop,
Boston, MA, 1901–c1920.

Peter L Krider
Philadelphia, PA, c1850–52.

Jacob Lansing
Albany, NY, 1681–1715.

Bartholomew Le Roux
New York, NY, 1681–1767.

Lincoln & Foss
Boston, MA, c1850–52.

Joseph Lownes
Philadelphia, PA, 1754–1816.

Marquand & Co.
New York, NY, c1835–40.

John McMullin
Philadelphia, PA, 1765–1843.

Monell & Williams
New York, NY, c1835–40.

John C Moore
New York, NY, c1832–40.

James Musgrave
Philadelphia, PA, c1793–1812.

Myer Myers
(1723–95) New York, NY.
Registered 1746, independent
maker by 1753.

John Owen Jnr.
Philadelphia, PA, c1804–30.

Pairpoint Manufacturing Co.
New Bedford, MA, 1880–.

Carl Poul Petersen
(1895–1977) Montreal, active
c1944–75. Born in Denmark and
apprenticed to George Jensen.
In 1922 he married Jensen's
daughter Inger and seven years
later they moved to Canada. He
worked as a master smith at Henry
Birks & Sons (see page 79) before
setting up a studio in 1939.

Reed & Barton
Taunton, MA. Isaac Babbitt began
a silversmiths in 1824; he was
joined by Henry G Reed and
Charles E Barton. By 1840 the
company was known as Reed &
Barton. It is still active today.

Paul Revere Snr.
Boston, MA, c1702–54.

Paul Revere Jnr.
(1735–1818) Son of Huguenot
silversmith, Paul Revere Snr.
Renowned for prodigious output
and varied life. A dramatic ride to
Lexington during the American
War of Independence on 19 April
1775 became the subject of a
poem by Longfellow.

Obadiah Rich
Boston, MA, c1830–50.

Joseph Richardson
Philadelphia, PA, 1711–85.

Robert Sanderson
(1608–93) Served his
apprenticeship with William
Rawlins in London, emigrated
to America c1640 and settled in
Boston, MA.

Savage, Lyman & Co.
Montreal, Canada, 1868–78.

John A Schanck
New York, NY, c1792–97.

Shreve, Brown & Co.
Boston, MA, c1856–58.

 Simons Bros.
Philadelphia, PA, 1839–.

Philemon Stacy Jnr.
Boston, MA, 1704–50.

 Arthur Stone
(1847–1938) c1857 apprenticed to silversmith in Sheffield, UK; 1884 emigrated to USA and worked in Concord, NH, for the Frank W Smith Silver Co. Inc. in Gardner, MA. He established his own shop in the town in 1901.

Philip Syng Jnr.
Philadelphia, PA, 1703–89.

John & Peter Targee
New York, NY, 1798–1810.

Barent Ten Eyck
Albany, NY, 1714–93.

Koenraet Ten Eyck
Albany, NY, 1703–50.

William Thomson
New York, NY, c1810–35.

Tiffany & Co.
(1837–) Founded by Charles Louis Tiffany (1812–1902) in New York, NY, and became one of America's most prestigious silver manufacturers.

R Wallace & Co.
Wallingford, CT, c1854–56.

Simon Wedge Snr.
(1774–1823) Baltimore, MD, 1798–1823.

Wilcox & Evertson
New York, NY, c1892–98.

R & W Wilson
Philadelphia, PA, c1825–85.

Christian Wiltberger
Philadelphia, PA, 1766–1851.

Hugh Wishart
New York, NY, c1785–1820.

Other American metalware

 The Handel Company
Founded by Philip Julius Handel in Meriden, CT, in 1876. The company made reverse-painted lamp shades, Tiffany-style leaded shades and other decorative objects. Closed in 1936.

 Roycroft
An Arts and Crafts community, East Aurora, NY, c1895. Copper shops built 1902 and made first commercial pieces 1906. Closed in 1938.

EUROPEAN SILVER MARKS

- Historically, because of almost constant wars between nations, Continental silver was frequently melted down to pay for armies and war debts.

- Europe used various standards but the only examples seen today are 800, 830 and 900 parts per thousand. These are usually shown by a small stamp. These do not necessarily correspond to contemporary English silver standards, and consequently objects with Continental marks are often sold as 'Continental silver', or 'silver-coloured metal'.

- Some European countries have developed a silver hallmarking system only very recently. Romania passed a law as recently as 1906 that silver must bear the maker's mark and a hallmark.

- The marks in this section consist of French and German silver marks, followed by other European marks in alphabetical order by country.

FRANCE

- In France, a form of guaranteeing marks was first used as early as 1272; however, despite the introduction of the silver standard in 1378, the system developed haphazardly and marking remained somewhat arbitrary.

- French silverwares may exhibit a community mark (confirming the standard of fineness), a maker's mark (usually consisting of his initials and emblem), a city mark and a juranda mark (the French equivalent of the British date letter system).

- A few other marks also appear. These include the charge mark, which appeared in 1672 and confirmed that any tax payable on the article had been noted and would be collected; the discharge mark confirms the payment of any such tax.

- Silver imported to France was stamped 'ET', for *étranger* (foreign). The recognition mark, introduced in 1750, was stamped on new parts added to old silver.

- From the 16thC, silver objects made in Paris were stamped with crowned letters by the wardens of the silversmiths' guild – La Maison Commune – who were responsible for maintaining the purity of silver. The letters changed annually with each warden (see page 84 for more details).

Community marks of the Paris Maison Commune

1697–1717	C–Z (no J or U)
1717–39	A–Z (no J or U)
1740–63	A–Z (no J or U)

1764–84	A–U (no J)
1784–89	P (in various sizes)

Examples of community marks

1729

1734

1752

1758

1764

1786

1789

1789

A similar crowned P mark in various styles used from 1784

Charge & discharge marks

- When silver was assayed (usually in parts) it was marked with a charge mark. This showed that the piece was of the required standard and duty was owed on the item.

- City charge marks were usually a letter – the letter for Paris was A – and their changing style can help with dating, although the marks are easily confused with some community marks used (see above). In the smaller provincial centres, a charge mark was often the town's arms or initials.

- When the tax owed was paid the piece was stamped with a discharge mark. Discharge marks also varied according to the region and often differ according to the size of the article.

- This system of marking was abolished in 1791, in the aftermath of the 1789 French Revolution. Control over the standard of silver was re-established in 1797. Tax was collected by the State from this date and silver was marked with a more uniform system.

City letter charge marks

A	Paris	G	Poitiers	N	Montpellier	T	Nantes	&	Aix
B	Rouen	H	La Rochelle	O	Riom	V	Troyes	AA	Metz
C	Caen	I	Limoges	P	Dijon	W	Lille	CC	Besançon
D	Lyons	K	Bordeaux	Q	Perpignan	X	Amiens	9	Rennes
E	Tours	L	Bayonne	R	Orléans	Y	Bourges		
F	Angers	M	Toulouse	S	Reims	Z	Grenoble		

(See individual city entries on following pages for facsimiles of city charge marks.)

Paris

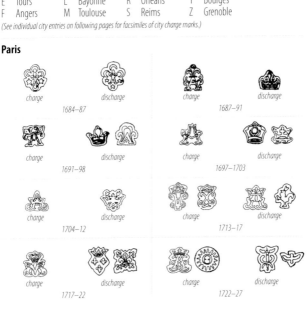

charge	*discharge*	*charge*	*discharge*
1684–87		*1687–91*	
charge	*discharge*	*charge*	*discharge*
	1691–98		*1697–1703*
charge	*discharge*	*charge*	*discharge*
	1704–12		*1713–17*
charge	*discharge*	*charge*	*discharge*
	1717–22		*1722–27*

European Silver – France

charge ... discharge
1727–32

charge ... discharge
1732–38

charge ... discharge
1738–44

charge ... discharge
1744–50

charge ... discharge
1750–56

charge ... discharge
1756–62

charge ... discharge
1762–68

charge ... discharge
1769–75

charge ... discharge
1775–81

charge ... discharge
1781–89

charge

discharge

1789

REGIONAL MARKS

Aix

charge
1750

charge   *discharge*

1774–80

charge   *discharge*

1780–90

charge   *discharge*

charge

discharge

1780–91

community
1780

Amiens

community
1737–39

charge
1764–74

discharge
1762–68

community
1768–74

community
1784–91

Angers

- Letter H surmounted by crown 1716–71.
- 'ANGERS' appears in 1748, 1750, 1754. It appears with letter 1774–83.

community
1716

discharge
1734–41

charge
1768–74

1774

1784–89

European Silver – France

Bordeaux

- Letter K in various styles surmounted by crown used as charge mark from 17thC until 1789.
- Various discharge marks used.
- Letters BOR with date letter appear in most community marks 17thC to early 18thC when it is replaced by the letter B and date letter.

charge	community	charge	community
1691–98	1691–98	1698–1703	1698–1703

charge	discharge	charge	discharge	community
1780–89		1780–89		1780

Dijon

- Letter P in various styles used as charge mark between the late 17thC and late 18thC.
- Discharge marks vary.

charge	discharge	charge	charge	discharge
1691–98	c1750	1756–59	1755–80	

charge	discharge
1784–91	

Grenoble
- Similar marks used between 1600 and 1760.
- Last two numbers of date used from c1784.

1716–18   *1741*   *1784–89*

Lille
- Similar mark or date letter surmounted by a crown used in 18thC.

1750   *1775*   *1770*

Lyons
- Letter D in various styles used as charge mark between the 17thC and the 1780s.
- Community mark shows lion rampant surmounted by crown with date letter 1712–77.
- Later marks vary.

charge   *discharge*   *charge*   *discharge*   *charge*   *discharge*   *community*
1775–80   *1780–91*   *1780–91*   *1776*

European Silver – France

Metz

- Shield with date letter used as a community mark in mid 18thC.

- AA or M used as a charge mark during late 18thC.

community mid 18thC	charge	discharge	charge	discharge
	1774–80		1780–91	

Montpellier

- Letters MP intertwined or letter N used for charge mark during 18thC.

- Date letter surmounted by a crown above letters MPL used as a community mark from 1709 to 1782.

community 1709	charge	discharge	charge	discharge	18thC
	1774–80		1780–89		

Nancy

- Similar mark used throughout 18thC.

c1790	late 18thC

Nantes

- Letter T used as a charge mark until mid 18thC when the word 'NANTES' appears within a shield.

discharge
1746

charge
1774

charge
1762–69

community
1772

Orléans

- Letter R used as a charge mark from 1732 until c1780.
- Various community marks used.

community
early 18thC

charge
1751–62

discharge

Poitiers

- Three Ps and a date letter used as a community mark during 18thC.
- Letter G surmounted by a crown in various styles used as charge mark between the 17thC and late 18thC.

community
1744

charge
1774–80

discharge

European Silver – France

Reims

- Letter S was mainly used as charge mark between c1768 and the late 18thC.
- Various community marks used.

community	*charge*	*discharge*	*community*	*community*
c1750	*1768–74*		*1768–74*	*1784–91*

Rennes

- Number nine in various styles used as charge mark between the late 17thC and late 18thC.

discharge	*community*	*community*	*charge*	*charge*	*discharge*
1721	*1725*	*1754–56*	*1756–62*	*1780–89*	

Riom

- Letter O used as charge mark during 18thC.
- Community marks vary.

community		*charge*	*discharge*
1775–80		*1780–89*	

La Rochelle
- Letters H or LR intertwined used as a charge mark.
- Various community marks used.

charge   *discharge*   *charge*   *discharge*   *community*

1774–80   *18thC*

Rouen
- Letter B surmounted by a crown used as a charge mark from the late 17thC.
- Letters surmounted by a crown used as a community mark.

charge   *discharge*   *community*

1774–80   *18thC*

Strasbourg
- Similar marks showing a shield surmounted with fleur-de-lys and number 13 used between the mid 17thC and 1796.
- Sometimes a crown surmounts the number.

1725   *1750–96*   *1752 date mark*   *1796*

European Silver – France

Toulouse

- Letter M used as charge mark from 16thC.
- Letters TOL surmounting a date letter in a shield used as a community mark between the late 17thC and the late 18thC.

charge
1768–74

community
1776

community
late 17thC–18thC

charge
1780–89

discharge

Tours

- Letter E surmounted by crown used as charge mark from early 18thC.
- Community marks show various crowned letters.

community
1739

charge
1768–74

charge
1774–80

discharge

discharge
1780–89

Later French marks

1793–94

1795–97

1797

1798

1798–1809

1809–19

1819–38

1879–

GERMANY

- Silver was marked in Germany from the 15thC.

- In Germany and Austria, a system was developed to denote the town of production, the maker and year letters, but these follow no reliable order. Similarly, although a silver standard existed in theory, it was not always strictly observed.

- German silver submitted for assay was marked to indicate its maker and town of origin. Town marks were often derived from the arms of the town or city in question.

- The two principal areas where goldsmithing had a long tradition were Nuremberg and Augsburg.

- Town marks changed slightly over the centuries and can help with dating. Nuremberg, Königsberg and Dresden also had date letter systems.

- There was no consistent purity guarantee for German silver before 1884. Since then, purity has been indicated in numbers, expressed as thousandths.

- In 1886, individual city marks were abolished and replaced by the national mark of a crescent moon and a crown, which represented a purity of at least .800. This mark became compulsory in 1888. It is used in conjunction with makers' marks and decimal purity.

- Purity mark for German silver 1888–

Augsburg

- Goldsmiths are recorded as early as the 13thC.

- The town mark (a pineapple) was introduced in 1529.

- Hallmarking seems to have died out in the mid 19thC.

1675–85   *1680–96*   *1712–13*   *1723–35*   *1723–35*   *Changeable letters represent a certain period, here 1787–89*

European Silver – Germany/Belgium

Dresden
- Variations on the crossed swords mark was used from the 18thC to mid 19thC.

early 18thC *late 18thC* *19thC*

Könisgsberg
- Similar mark used between the late 17th and mid 19thC.

early 18thC *mid 18thC* *c1815*

Nuremberg
- Pieces were hallmarked as early as the late 14thC.
- The town mark (the letter N) and a system of recording makers' marks was in use by 1541.

late 18thC *early 19thC*

Date letters

1766–69 *1769–73* *1773–76* *1776–80* *1780–83* *1783–87* *1787–90* *1790–94* *1794–97* *1797–1800*

BELGIUM
- Silversmiths in Brussels, Artois (Northern France, now Belgium), Luxembourg and the Netherlands were regulated from the mid 16thC by order of Emperor Charles V.
- By the 17thC, silver was marked with a town mark, date letter and maker's mark.
- Hallmarking became obligatory in 1831.
- After 1869, assaying was no longer customary.

Hallmarks used 1814–31

Large objects	*Small objects*	

Large objects   *Small objects*

Hallmarks used 1831–68

.950   *.800*

Purity

Large objects   *Small objects*

Hallmark

Hallmarks used 1869–1942

.900   *.800*

Large objects

.900   *.800*

Small objects

Hallmarks used from 1942–

Large objects

Small objects

DENMARK

- Danish silver was marked with a city or town mark from the 17thC.

- From the late 17thC, silver had four marks: town mark; assayer's mark (usually his initials in a square or oval cartouche); mark of the month (sign of the zodiac); and maker's mark.

- Copenhagen's mark usually incorporates the date.

SILVER

- From 1888, Danish silver of a purity of .826 was stamped with an official mark showing the three towers of Copenhagen in an oval and the last two numbers of the year the piece was assayed.

.826 purity

ITALY

- A uniform system of marking began in 1810 when assay offices were established in Milan, Venice, Ancona, Verona and Brescia. Before this, many towns adopted their own hallmarks.

- From 1873, hallmarking was adopted throughout the country.

- Purity was not obligatory but marks denoting purities of .950, .900 and .800 were used.

- New standards of .925 and .800 were introduced in 1935.

Florence

17th–18thC

18thC

Rome

17thC

late 18thC

Turin

18th–19thC

Modern silver marks (1934–)

THE NETHERLANDS

- From the mid 17thC, silver was marked with maker's mark, date letter, town mark, assayer's mark and a hallmark showing the crowned lion, which guaranteed the purity of .875.

- New purity standards of .934 and .833 were used between 1806 and 1810.

- The Netherlands adopted French marking systems from 1811 until 1953.

Assay office marks

Amsterdam	Arnhem	Den Bosch	Delft	Dordrecht

Gouda	The Hague	Rotterdam	Utrecht	Zwolle

Purity marks used 1810–14

large .950   *.800*   *small .800*

Purity marks used 1814–1953

large .934   *.833*   *small .833*

European Silver – The Netherlands/Norway

Dutch date letters 1814–1949
- A standard national system of date letters was used from 1814. The letters below are the first and last examples of each alphabet set (A–Z).

1814   *1834*   *1835*   *1859*   *1860*   *1884*   *1885*   *1909*

1910   *1934*   *1935*   *1944–45*   *1945–47*   *1948–July*   *July–1949*

Marks on silver from 1953–

large .925   *.835*   *small .835*   *.800*

NORWAY

- Early Norwegian marks usually comprised a city mark and the date (or a letter designating the year).
- From the mid 17thC to the mid 18thC, silver production was controlled by the king and the guilds were abolished.
- From 1766, silver was marked with a monthly mark, expressed either as a fraction or as a sign of the zodiac.

Date marks
- During the 19thC, date marks sometimes appear in full or are shown by the last two numbers of the year.

1802   *1832*   *1843*

100

Monthly marks

- From 1740 to 1765, monthly marks were shown as signs of the zodiac.
- From 1766 to 1820, fractions of 12 showed the month.

| Dec 21–Jan 21 | Jan 21–Feb 18 | Feb 18–Mar 20 | Mar 20–Apr 20 | Apr 20–May 21 | May 22–June 21 |

June 21–July 22   July 22–Aug 21   Aug 21–Sept 23   Sept 23–Oct 23   Oct 23–Nov 22   Nov 22–Dec 21

Purity marks used 1893–

purity .830–.925   .830–.925

PORTUGAL

- Before 1881, Portuguese silver was marked with a maker's mark and a town mark, which guaranteed a purity of .958.
- Town marks usually consisted of the first letter of the town concerned within a shield of varying form.
- State hallmarking was introduced in 1881 and purity standards of .916 and .833 were obligatory from 1886.
- New hallmarking systems were introduced in 1938 and continue to this day.

Lisbon

- Letter L used in shields of varying shape between the late 17thC and late 19thC.

large 17thC   *early 18thC*   *early 19thC*

Oporto

- Letter P used in shields of varying shape between the late 17thC and late 19thC.

late 17thC   *early 18thC*   *1791–1810*   *1836–43*

Purity marks used 1886–1938

Lisbon and Oporto

large .916   *.833*   *small .916*   *.833*

Marks used 1938–

Lisbon and Oporto

RUSSIA

- In medieval Russia, every large monastic foundation had its own silversmith and from the 17thC onwards all silver belonging to the patriarchs was stamped with the blessing hand.

- From 1613, all silver sold at fairs had to be marked and, in 1700, a gold and silver standard was introduced to be overseen by assay offices established in all Russian towns.

- In Moscow, silver had been marked from 1613. The first mark showed a two-headed eagle. In 1684, the eagle was replaced with a purity mark and date mark inside a circle. The eagle returned to use from 1700 to 1710 and carried a sceptre and orb.

- Assay offices were established in Moscow and St Petersburg during the first half of the 18thC.

- Throughout the 18thC and 19thC, silver made in Moscow or St Petersburg was marked by the maker, the guild and the assay office, where it was stamped with the mark of the assayer and the office.

- From 1729 in Moscow, the date was stamped separately and the assayer's initials were marked beneath the eagle. From 1733 the word 'MOCKBA' appeared under the eagle. After 1741, a new mark showing St George killing the dragon was introduced.

- Provincial silver was marked with the town mark, maker's mark and a mark of purity in figures in a rectangular shield. A comprehensive system of marking was introduced in 1891; this included the initials of the assayer and a woman's head.

Purity marks used 1882–

National mark 1896–   *National mark 1908–17*   *National mark 1927–58*

SPAIN

- From the 16thC, silver was marked with a maker's mark and a town mark. According to royal decree, only silver of a purity of .930 was admissible.

- Date marks began to be used in certain towns at the end of the 18thC.

- Two lower standards were established in 1881 and silver could be assayed on request.

- From 1934, items were stamped with a maker's mark and a mark of purity.

Assay marks 1881–

.750

.916

SWEDEN

- By the 16thC, Swedish silver was marked with both a maker's mark and a town mark.
- Date letters were introduced during the late 17thC in Stockholm.
- During the mid 18thC, the State controlled the purity of silver objects.
- A comprehensive date letter system was adopted throughout Sweden and Finland from 1758.
- From 1860, different assay offices adopted letter marks.

Stockholm

- Crown mark used from c1690 to c1715, when it was replaced by crowned head until c1850.

late 17th–early 18thC   *18th–19thC*

City marks 1912–

From 1912 the town's initial letter was used.

Åhus   *Gäfle*   *Karlstad*   *Malmö*   *Nora*   *Sala*   *Ystad*

Date letters (the alphabet excluding J and W)

A-Z	1759-82	A5-Z5	1855-78	A9-Z9	1951-74
A2-Z2	1783-1806	A6-Z6	1879-1902	A10-Z10	1975-98
A3-Z3	1807-30	A7-Z7	1903-26	A11-Z11	1999-2022
A4-Z4	1831-54	A8-Z8	1927-50		

SWITZERLAND

- The standards of purity were regulated in Zurich, Lucerne and Basle from the mid 16thC. Each canton adopted its own mark, usually a pictorial symbol with or without an initial.
- Uniform purity in five standards – .935, .925, .900, .875 and .800 – was adopted from 1848.
- Uniform marks were adopted from 1882.

Geneva
- Similar mark used between 17thC and late 18thC.

17thC *late 18thC* *19thC*

Zurich

- Letter Z in a shield used between the 16thC and 18thC.

16th–18thC

Marks used 1882–1934

large .875 *.800*

SHEFFIELD PLATE

- The craft of covering a base metal with a precious metal, known as close plating, has been practised for centuries.

- In the mid 18thC, a commercially viable variation (later known as Sheffield plate) allowed the large-scale production of plated wares for domestic use.

- Sheffield plate was formed from thin sheets of silver and copper. The secret of its success was that it could be used to produce a host of items at a fraction of the cost of solid silver.

- After the 1840s and the advent of electroplating, materials other than copper were used as the base body material, the most popular being nickel.

- The greatest areas of production in the UK were Sheffield and Birmingham. Matthew Boulton (Birmingham) was one of the most famous manufactories.

- Early Sheffield plate was rarely marked, if at all. In 1784, legislation was introduced that allowed for a maker's mark and device. The practice of marking became more common as the century progressed.

- It was not until the late 18thC that a set of marks began to appear, which were dangerously similar to those applied to sterling silver. The Plate Assay (Sheffield and Birmingham) Act of 1772 ordered these two assay offices to ensure that no marks applied to plated goods should resemble too closely those on silver.

- By the 1840s, a crown, a fleur-de-lys and other symbols were added, set in a straight line. During the late 19thC, the letters EPNS (electroplated nickel silver) and EPBM (electroplated Britannia metal) appeared, very often disguised or made to look like hallmarks.

BOULTON ❀	M Boulton & Co.
C෴PE෴	C G Cope
▦ ▦ ◉ ▩	T & J Creswick
G&R DIXON'S IMPERIAL	J Dixon & Sons
DIXON&C෴	T Dixon & Co.
ELL ER BY ❖	W Ellerby
▦ ◈ ◉ ◈ HF	H Freeth
	W Garnett

Mark	Maker
	J Gilbert
HALL	W Hall
IOS⁴ HANCOCK SHEFFIELD.	Joseph Hancock
	T Harwood
HOLLAND & C°	H Holland & Co.
S H & C° / Howard	S & T Howard
Hutton / H & S T	W Hutton
R.LAW. J	R Law
A·C·LEA	A C Lea
J·LOVE·&·C°	J Love & Co.
MER EDITH	H Meredith
MOORE	J Moore
J&S ROBERTS	J & S Roberts
	Cadman Roberts & Co.
Sil-kirk	W Silkirk
	Smith Robarts & Co.
H T & C°	Tudor & Leader
	Tudor & Leader
	Hatfield Waterhouse & Co.
	J Watson & Son
DAN¹ HOLY WILKINSON & C°	D Holy Wilkinson & Co.
WOOD WARD	W Woodward
WRIGHT FAIRBAIRN	J Wright & G Fairbairn
S.C.YOUNGE & C°	S & C Younge & Co.

107

GOLD

GOLD

- Gold is alloyed, most often with silver or copper, in order to harden it.

- The standard marks for sterling silver and gold were the same until 1798.

- In 1300, the first legal standard for gold was set at 19⅕ carats of pure gold to 24, a carat being the 24th part weight of the whole – i.e. an item of gold had to contain a minimum of 19⅕ parts of pure gold per 24. The standard was indicated by a leopard's head.

- The maker's mark was required from 1363 and a date letter from 1578.

- In 1477, the standard was reduced to 18 carats. In 1575 it became 22 carats: a standard that still applies today.

- From 1544, the standard mark was a lion passant.

- When the lower 18-carat standard was readmitted as a legal standard in 1798, it was shown by a crown. From 1844, the crown mark was used for both standards.

- The sun mark was briefly used on 22-carat gold assayed in London between May 1816 and the introduction of the crown mark in 1844.

- In 1854, three more standards were established – 15, 12 and 9 carat – and the specific quality of the gold was indicated by both a figure and a percentage. In 1932, the 12- and 15-carat standards were dropped and replaced by the 14-carat standard.

	To 1974		1975–		foreign imports	
22 carat	🛡	22	☀	916	⬠	916
18 carat	🛡	18	☀	750	⬡	750
14 carat	🛡	585	☀	585	⬡	585
9 carat	🛡	375	☀	375	⬡	375

Scottish offices used the following marks in the place of the crown:

Edinburgh

 Glasgow

Assay office marks

London

Newcastle

Glasgow

Birmingham

Sheffield

Dublin

Chester

York

Exeter

Edinburgh

BRONZE

Chryselephantine figure
of a dancer as Semiramis,
by Demetre Chiparus

- Many bronze or chryselephantine (bronze and ivory) figures are signed by the artist and by the foundry. This can be a strong indicator of value as the work of some sculptors is more sought after than the work of others.

- Important sculptors include Demetre Chiparus, Pierre Le Faguays (Fayral), Claire Jeanne Roberte Colinet and Bruno Zach.

- Signed work is always desirable, but the quality of the work is more important and the value of a poor-quality casting is not increased by the presence of a signature.

- Signatures may appear on the base or be cast in the bronze.

- The marks in this section are organized in alphabetical order by surname or foundry name.

Bronze sculptors

Barbedienne (foundry)
French
1838–1952

Paul-Albert Bartholomé
French
1848–1928

Antoine-Louis Barye
French
1796–1875

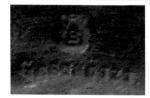

Franz Xaver Bergmann
Austrian
1861–1936

Suzanne Bizard
French
1873–1963

Émile Victor Blavier
French
1852–1876

Eugen Börmel
German
1858–1932

Eutrope Bouret
French
1833–1906

Maurice Bouval
French
1863–1916

Thomas-François Cartier
French
1879–1943

Louis Chalon
French
1866–1916

Demetre Chiparus
Romanian
1886–1947

Clodion (Claude Michel)
French
1738–1814

Claire Jeanne Roberte Colinet
Belgian
1852–1908

Alfred Drury
British
1859–1944

Ludwig Eisenberger
German
1895–1920

**La Société Anonyme
Edmond Etling**
French
1909–1945

Emmanuel Frémiet
French
1824–1910

Ignacio Gallo
Spanish
d.1935

Jean Garnier
French
1853–1910

Adrien Gaudez
French
1845–1902

August Gaul
German
1869–1921

Gerda Iro Gerdago
Austrian
1906–2004

Friedrich Gornik
Austrian
1877–1943

Franz Iffland
German
1862–1935

Rudolf Kaesbach
German
1873–1955

Carl Kauba
Austrian
1865–1922

Jonathan Knight
British
b.1954

Pierre Le Faguays (Fayral / Guerbe)
French
1892–1935

Agathon Léonard (Léonard Agathon van Weydevelt)
French
1841–1923

Josef Lorenzl
Austrian
1892–1950

Eugene Marioton
French
1854–1925

Émile Manz
German
1880–1945

Alois Mayer
German
1855–1939

Pierre Jules Mêne
French
1810–79

Mathurin Moreau
French
1822–1912

Erich Oehme
German
1889–1970

Georges Omerth
French
1895–1925

Alexandre Ouline
Belgian
Active 1918–40

113

Hans Parzinger
German
1800–1900

Victor Peter
French
1840–1918

Paul Philippe
French
1870–1930

Rudolf Podany
Austrian
1876–1963

Otto Rasmussen
German
b.1845

Francis Renaud
French
1887–1973

Louis Riché
French
1877–1949

Wilhelm Carl Robra
German
1876–1945

Emy Roeder-Garbe
German
1890–1971

Franz Rosse
French
1858–1900

**Charles
Marion
Russell**
American
1864–1926

Léopold Savine
French
1861–1934

**Nikolaus
Outzen
Schmidt**
Danish
1844–1910

Otto Schmidt-Hofer
German
1873–1925

Ernst Seger
German
1868–1939

Victor Heinrich Seifert
Austrian
1870–1953

Etienne Alexandre Stella
French
d.1892

Georges van der Straeten
Belgian
1856–1928

Prince Paul Troubetzkoy
Russian
1866–1938

Alexandre Vibert
French
1847–1909

Johann Vierthaler
German
1869–1957

Bruno Zach
Austrian
1891–1935

CERAMICS

Pilkington's vase, painted by
William S Mycock

INTRODUCTION TO CERAMIC MARKS

Although many pieces of ceramic are unmarked, marks are a very important tool in helping to establish the date, company and place of manufacture. It is important to realize that marks can be copied or faked and many simple marks, such as letters, have been used by more than one factory. For example, the Worcester crescent mark was also used by Bow, Lowestoft and Caughley. Some famous marks were deliberately copied by other factories hoping to emulate the success of their competitors. The crossed swords mark is famously used by the premier European factory, Meissen, but it was also used, at some stage, by most other European factories.

Chinese porcelain is virtually impossible to date from the reign mark alone as few pieces bear the mark of the reign they were produced in. Some are forgeries but many are marked with older reign marks as a device for the Chinese potters to venerate their ancestors.

Remember that identifying and dating pottery and porcelain from marks is an erratic and inexact science. The marks contained in this chapter should be seen as the start of a journey of discovery rather than the end. There are, however, some useful general rules.

SOME HELPFUL CLUES TO DATING

- Pattern numbers began to appear at the end of the 18thC.

- A piece printed with the name of a pattern is unlikely to date from before 1800.

- A mark with 'Ltd.' after the company name would not be pre-1860 and is most likely found after 1880.

- The use of 'Rd. No.' followed by a run of numbers indicates a date after 1884.

- The use of the word 'Royal' indicates a date after 1850.

- If a country name, such as 'Germany', 'Bavaria', 'England', is included, the piece dates from after 1891. Pieces marked 'Made in Germany' or 'Made in England' are most likely 20thC.

- The 'Bone China' mark was not used until the 20thC.

WHAT IS IN THIS CHAPTER?

The range of material covered in this chapter includes the most common Chinese reign marks, European and American factory marks and designers' marks. The proliferation of factories in the 19thC and 20thC renders it impossible to include them all, as many of these factories were either short-lived or relatively unimportant. Well-established manufacturers often made changes to their trademarks and to include all the variations would occupy more space than is available here.

The marks have been included in the most logical order possible, but this has not always proved to be straightforward. It is worth checking in the different sections if the mark proves to be elusive. Always check if there is a main factory name present in the mark and use the index to find other marks by the same factory.

HOW TO FIND YOUR CERAMIC MARK

This chapter has been ordered by type of mark.

- Pages 120–22: Chinese Marks, ordered chronologically.

- Pages 123–45: Marks containing letters, ordered alphabetically by the letters shown in the mark and then alphabetically by factory.

- Pages 146–85: Marks containing the factory or designer's names, ordered alphabetically by the name shown on the mark. For example, Alfred Meakin Ltd. is listed under 'A'.

- Pages 186–97: Marks without names or letters, ordered by type of device used and then alphabetically by factory. The devices are arranged in the following order: Swords pages 186–87; Crowns pages 188–89; Stars & Crosses pages 190–91; Animals pages 191–92; Shields page 192; Anchors page 193; Circles page 194; Crescents page 194; Fleur-de-lys page 195; Plants page 195; Scrolls page 196; Triangles page 196; Other Devices pages 196–97.

- Pages 198–99: Marks of studio potters, ordered by surname.

- Pages 200–20: Dating and identification charts. Design Registration Marks pages 200–01; Derby Dating Codes page 202; Minton Dating Codes page 203; Newcomb Decorators' Marks page 204; Rookwood Dating and Decorators' Marks pages 205–07; Sèvres Dating and Decorators' Marks pages 208–18; Wedgwood Dating Codes pages 218–19; Worcester Dating Codes pages 219–20.

Chinese Reign Marks

Early periods & dates

Sui Dynasty 581–618

Tang Dynasty 618–906

Five Dynasties 907–60

Song Dynasty 960–1279

Jin Dynasty 1115–1234

Yuan Dynasty 1260–1368

Some earlier Ming Dynasty reigns

Hongwu 1368–98

Jianwen 1399–1402

Yongle 1403–24

Hongxi 1425

Ming Dynasty marks

Xuande
1426–35

Chenghua
1465–87

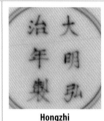

Hongzhi
1488–1505

Zhengde
1506–21

Jiajing
1522–66

Wanli
1573–1619

Chongzhen
1628–44

Qing Dynasty marks

熙 大 年 清 製 康	年 大 雍 清 製 正	隆 大 年 清 製 乾
Kangxi *1662–1722*	**Yongzheng** *1723–35*	**Qianlong** *1736–95*

年 嘉 製 慶	豐 大 年 清 製 咸	治 大 年 清 製 同
Jiaqing *1796–1820*	**Xianfeng** *1851–61*	**Tongzhi** *1862–74*

緒 大 年 清 製 光	統 大 年 清 製 宣	御 洪 製 憲
Guangxu *1875–1908*	**Xuantong** *1909–11*	**Hongxian** *1915–16*

Chinese Zhuanshu Script Marks

Chinese reign marks on the base can be made up of four to six Chinese characters, in *kaishu* (normal script) or *zhuanshu* (archaic seal script). *Zhuanshu* was developed from bronze inscriptions and stylized into a form of calligraphy.

Jiajing
1522–66

Kangxi
1662–1722

Yongzheng
1723–35

Qianlong
1736–95

Daoguang
1821–50

Xianfeng
1851–61

Tongzhi
1862–74

Amphora Porzellanfabrik
/ Reissner, Stellmacher & Kessel
Turn-Templitz, Bohemia
1894–

Ansbach
Bavaria, Germany
1758–1860

Longton Hall
Staffordshire, UK
c1749–60

St Petersburg
Russia
1744–1917
This mark 1801–25

Arkinstall & Sons Ltd.
Stoke-on-Trent,
Staffordshire, UK
'Arcadian' trade name mark
1904–24

Fouque-Arnoux & Cie.
Valentine, Haute-Garonne, France
1832–60

A G Harley Jones
Fenton, Staffordshire,
UK
1907–34
This mark 1923–34

Höchst
Nr. Mainz, Germany
1746–
This mark for painter
Adam Ludwig c1749–58

Albert Potteries Ltd.
Burslem, Staffordshire,
UK
1946–54

CERAMICS

Aylesford Priory Pottery
Aylesford, Kent, UK
1955–

Aprey
Haute-Marne, France
c1744–

Meissen
Nr. Dresden,
Saxony,
Germany
1710–
*This mark
Augustus Rex
monogram
1723–40*

Alexander Popoff
Gorbunovo, Nr. Moscow,
Russia
c1810–72

American Encaustic Tiling Company
Zanesville, OH, USA
1875–1935

Booths Ltd.
Tunstall, Staffordshire, UK
c1891–1948
This mark 1905–20s

Bow China
Stratford, London, UK
c1747–76
This mark 1750s

Bing & Grøndahl
Copenhagen, Denmark
1853–

This mark 1853–95

This mark 1948–52

Burroughs & Mountford
Trenton, NJ, USA
1879–95

Niderviller
Lorraine, France
1765–
This mark Baron de
Beyerlé 1765–70

A B Jones & Sons
Longton, Staffordshire, UK
1900–72
This mark 1900–13

Britannia China Co.
Longton, Staffordshire, UK
1895–1906
This mark 1904–06

Bremer & Schmidt
Eisenberg, Thuringia,
Germany
1895–1972

**Wilcox & Co. Ltd.
/ Burmantofts**
Leeds, Yorkshire, UK
1882–1904

**Birks, Rawlins
& Co. Ltd.**
Stoke, Staffordshire, UK
1896–1933
This mark 1900–

**Worcester
Porcelains**
Worcester, UK, *1751–*
This mark Barr, Flight &
Barr c1807–13

**C J C Bailey
/ Bailey & Co.**
Fulham, London, UK
1864–89

**Burgess & Leigh
Ltd.**
Burslem, Staffordshire, UK
1862–

Nymphenburg
Bavaria, Germany
1747–

Bernard Moore
Stoke, Staffordshire, UK
1905–15

**Blue Mountain
Pottery**
Collingwood, ON,
Canada
1953–2004

Brown-Westhead, Moore & Co.
Hanley, Staffordshire, UK
1862–1904
This mark c1895–1904

Bayreuth
Bavaria, Germany
1719–1835
This mark for proprietor
Johann Georg Pfeiffer 1760–67

Schomberg & Söhne
Teltow, Prussia, Germany
1853–
This mark 1906–11

Bayeux
Calvados, Normandy, France
1810–1951
This mark 1878–1945

Caughley / Salopian
Brosley, Shropshire, UK
c1750–99
This mark 1775–99

Coalport Porcelain
Coalport, Shropshire, UK
c1795–
This mark c1845–55

Höchst
Nr. Mainz, Germany
1746–
This mark for painter
Lothar Charlot c1748

A T Safronoff
Moscow, Russia
c1830–40

Robert Wilson
Hanley, Staffordshire, UK
1795–1801

Worcester Porcelains
Worcester, UK
c1751–
This mark c1755–90

Ludwigsburg
Württemberg, Germany
1758–1824

These marks 1758–93   *This mark 1776–1824*

Sèvres
France
1756–
Mark used 1824–30
This mark 1825

Cartwright & Edwards
Fenton, Staffordshire, UK
c1857–1955
This mark c1900–

Cincinnati Art Pottery
Cincinnati, OH, USA
1879–91

Carl Schumann
Arzberg, Bavaria, Germany
1881–1994
This mark 1892–1923

C C Thompson Pottery Co.
East Liverpool, OH, USA
1868–1938

Limoges
Haute-Vienne, France
1771–96
This mark for the Comte D'Artois

Charles Fergus Binns
Alfred, New York, NY, USA
1900–35

Chelsea Keramic Art / Dedham
Dedham, MA, USA
1870s–1943
This mark 1875–1943

Caen
Calvados, Normandy, France
1793–1806
This mark 1799–1806

Carter, Stabler & Adams Ltd.
Poole Pottery, Dorset, UK
1921–

Carl Thieme
Potschappel, Dresden, Germany
1872–

Frankenthal
Palatinate, Germany
1755–99

This mark for Carl Theodor 1762–88

This mark for Carl Theodor 1780–93

C T Maling & Sons Ltd.
Newcastle upon Tyne, Northumberland, UK
1762–1963
This mark c1900

Charles Vyse
Cheyne Row, London, UK
1919–63
This mark 1922

De Pauw (The Peacock)
Delft, Holland
1652–1779

Chelsea-Derby Porcelain
London, UK
c1769–84

Derby Porcelain
Derbyshire, UK
c1750–
This mark c1782–1825
In red c1806–25

Derby Porcelain
Derbyshire, UK
c1750–
This mark
c1782–c1800

Helena Wolfsohn
Dresden, Germany
c1843–83
This mark c1843–78

Thomas Dimmock Jnr. & Co.
Shelton and Hanley, Staffordshire, UK
c1828–59

Dahl-Jensens, Jens Peter
Copenhagen, Denmark
1925–84

William De Morgan
London, UK
c1872–1907
This mark 1882–

Della Robbia Co. Ltd.
Birkenhead, Cheshire, UK
1894–1901

Daniel & James Franklin Seagle
Vale, NC, USA
1828–88

Edge Malkin & Co. Ltd.
Burslem, Staffordshire, UK
1871–1903

East Liverpool Pottery Co.
East Liverpool, OH, USA
1894–1901

Fürstenberg
Brunswick, Germany
c1753–
This mark c1753–80

Hanau
Frankfurt-am-Main,
Germany
1661–1806
This mark 1740–87

Ludwigsburg
Württemberg, Germany
1758–1824
This mark 1806–16

Thomas Fell & Co.
Newcastle upon Tyne, UK
c1817–90
This mark 1817–30

Worcester Porcelains
Worcester, UK
c1751–
This mark Flight,
Barr & Barr
c1813–40

Höchst
Nr. Mainz, Germany
1746–
This mark for artist
Georg Friedrich Hess

Bayreuth
Bavaria, Germany
1719–1835
This mark for decorator
J F Metzsch 1735–51

Berlin / Gotzkowsky
Germany
1761–c1763
This mark 1761–63

Gardner Porcelain
Nr. Moscow, Russia
c1765–1891

Gera
Thuringia, Germany
c1752–80

Ginori Factory
Doccia, Tuscany, Italy
1735–
This mark 1874–88

Gotha
Thuringia, Germany
1757–1937
This mark c1802–34

James Neale & Co.
Hanley, Staffordshire, UK
c1776–86

Unger, Schneider & Hutschenreuther
Gräfenthal, Thuringia, Germany
1861–86

Gater, Hall & Co.
Burslem, Staffordshire, UK
c1899–1943
This mark 1914–43

George Jones & Sons Ltd.
Stoke-on-Trent, Staffordshire, UK
c1864–1957
This mark c1924–51

G M Creyke & Sons
Hanley, Staffordshire, UK
1920–48

This mark 1920–c1930

This mark 1930–48

George Procter & Co. Ltd.
Longton, Staffordshire, UK
1891–1940
This mark 1924–40

Grove & Stark
Longton, Staffordshire, UK
1871–85

CERAMICS

Griffen, Smith & Hill
Phoenixville, PA, USA
1882–94

George Warrilow & Sons Ltd.
Longton, Staffordshire, UK
1887–1940

Brunswick
Germany
1707–49
This mark 1710–49

Höchst
Nr. Mainz, Germany
1746–
This mark for artist Georg Friedrich Hess

Pierre-Antoine Hannong
Faubourg Saint-Denis, Paris, France
1771–1828

The Imperial Factory St Petersburg
St Petersburg, Russia
1744–1917
This mark c1825–55

Harrop & Burgess
Hanley, Staffordshire, UK
1894–1903

Hibbert & Boughley
Longton, Staffordshire, UK
Late 19thC
This mark 1889–

Hammersley & Co.
Longton, Staffordshire, UK
1887–1932
This mark 1887–1912

Heath & Greatbatch
Burslem, Staffordshire, UK
1891–93

Hilditch & Son
Lane End, Staffordshire,
UK
1822–30

**Harvey Adams
& Co.**
Longton, Staffordshire,
UK
1870–85

**De Drie Porceleyne
Flessies**
Delft, Holland
1764–77
Mark for potter H Brouwer

**Oldswinford
Pottery**
Stourbridge, UK
1955–60
*This mark for potter
Howard Bissell*

Quimper
Quimper, France
c1690–
*This mark for A de la
Hubaudière 1782–94*

Kelsterbach
Hessen-Darmstadt,
Germany
c1761–1802
This mark 1799–1802

**Sutherland
Pottery**
Staffordshire, UK
1865–1940
*This mark for Joseph
Holdcroft 1865–1906*

Linthorpe Pottery
Middlesbrough, UK
1879–89
*This mark for artist Henry
Tooth 1879–83*

Hutschenreuther
Selb, Bavaria,
Germany
c1856–
This mark c1891–

Tooth & Co. Ltd.
Woodville, Derbyshire, UK
1883–1996
*This mark for proprietor
Henry Tooth 1883–1900*

Jersey City Pottery
Jersey City, NJ, USA
c1850–92

Ilmenauer Porzellanfabrik Graf von Henneberg AG
Ilmenauer, Thuringia, Germany
1777–1945 This mark c1900

Jaeger, Thomas & Co.
Marktredwitz, Bavaria, Germany
c1872–c1979
This mark 1898–1923

J B Owens Pottery Co.
Zanesville, OH, USA
1896–1907

John Denton Baxter
Hanley, Staffordshire, UK
1823–27
This mark includes a Staffordshire knot

J Goodwin Stoddard & Co.
Longton, Staffordshire, UK
1898–1940
This mark 1898–1936

Joseph Hannong
Strasbourg, France and Frankenthal, Palatinate, Germany
c1760–80

Julius Hering & Söhn
Köppelsdorf, Thuringia, Germany
1893–

Ansbach
Bavaria, Germany
c1758–1860
This mark for proprietor Johann Popp c1758–92

CERAMICS

Glasgow Pottery
Trenton, NJ, USA
1863–1900
John Moses & Sons from 1900–05

Ilmenauer Porzellanfabrik Graf von Henneberg AG
Ilmenauer, Thuringia, Germany
1777–1945 This mark 1903–30

Jacob Petit
Fontainebleau, Seine-et-Marne, France
1795–
This mark c1830–60

James S Taft & Co. / Hampshire Pottery Co.
Keene, NH, USA
1871–1923

Höchst
Nr. Mainz, Germany
1746–
This mark for artist Johannes Zeschinger

Edwin M Knowles China Co.
East Liverpool, OH, USA
1900–63

Karl Richard Klemm
Dresden, Germany
c1869–1940s
This mark c1891–

Knowles, Taylor & Knowles
East Liverpool, OH, USA
1870–1929

Meissen
Nr. Dresden, Saxony, Germany
1710–
This mark c1720s

Royal Porcelain Factory Berlin
Berlin, Germany
1763–

This mark 1832–

This mark 1837–44

This mark 1844–47

Kloster Veilsdorf
Thuringia, Germany
1760–
This mark c1760–97

Ludwigsburg
Württemberg, Germany
1758–1824
This mark 1793–95

De Lampetkan
Delft, Holland
1637–c1810
This mark c1800–10

Middle Lane Pottery
New York, NY, USA
1894–1932
Mark for potter T Brouwer

Minton
Stoke-on-Trent, Staffordshire, UK
1793–
This mark c1800–30

Mayer & Elliott
Longport, Staffordshire, UK
1858–61

Mayer & Sherratt
Longton, Staffordshire, UK
1906–41

CERAMICS

Buen Retiro
Madrid, Spain
1759–
This mark 1804–50

Morley Fox & Co. Ltd.
Fenton,
Staffordshire, UK
1906–44
This mark c1906

Faïence Manufacturing Co.
New York, NY, USA
1880–92

Maestro Giorgio Andreoli
Gubbio, Italy
c1492–1541

Metzler & Ortloff
Thuringia, Germany
1875–1976
This mark 1926–72

Oude Loosdrecht
Holland
1771–82

Marblehead Pottery
Marblehead, MA, USA
1904–36

Middlesbrough Pottery Co.
Yorkshire, UK
c1834–44

Marzi & Remy
Hesse-Nassau, Germany
1880–1994
This mark 1964–94

Morris & Willmore
Trenton, NJ, USA
1893–1905

Ginori Factory
Doccia, Tuscany, Italy
1735–
This mark 1850–1905

137

CERAMICS

Naples
Italy
1771–1834

Niderviller
Lorraine, France
1765–

Nuremberg
Bavaria, Germany
16thC–
This mark 1750–

Newcomb College
New Orleans, LA, USA
1895–1940

New England Pottery Co.
East Boston, MA, USA
1854–1914
This mark 1883–86

New Jersey Pottery Co.
Trenton, NJ, USA
1869–83

New Milford Pottery Co. / Wannopee Pottery
New Milford, CT, USA
1886–1903

Joseph Olerys
Moustiers, Basse-Alpes, France
c1738–

Onondaga Pottery
Syracuse, NY, USA
1871–1966

Ollivant Potteries Ltd.
Stoke-on-Trent,
Staffordshire, UK
1948–54

Ott & Brewer / Etruria Pottery
Trenton, NJ, USA
1863–1993

Bonnin & Morris
Philadelphia, PA, USA
1769–72

Pilkington's Tile & Pottery Co. Ltd.
Clifton Junction, Nr. Manchester, UK
c1897–1938 and 1948–57

This mark 1904–05

This mark 1922–38

Count Leopold von Proskau
Silesia, Germany
1763–c1850
This mark 1783–93

Powell & Bishop / Powell, Bishop & Stonier
Hanley, Staffordshire, UK
1878–91

Casa Pirota
Faenza, Emilia, Italy
16thC

139

Frankenthal
Palatinate, Germany
1755–62

This mark for director Paul Hannong

This mark for director Pierre-Antoine Hannong

This mark for director Paul Hannong

Paul Revere Pottery/Saturday Evening Girls
Boston, Brighton, MA, USA
1907–42

Roseville Pottery Co.
Roseville and Zanesville, OH, USA
1890–1954

Joseph Rieber & Co.
Mitterteich, Germany
1868–
This mark 1945–71

Karl Friedrich Lüdicke
Rheinsberg, Brandenburg, Germany
1762–1866

Rauenstein
Thuringia, Germany
1783–1901
This mark 1783–1820

Rörstrand
Sweden
1726–2005
This mark 20thC

Rosenthal
Selb, Bavaria, Germany
1879–
This mark for designer Raymond Loewy 1950s

William Ratcliffe
Hanley, Staffordshire, UK
c1831–40

Redfern & Drakeford Ltd.
Longton, Staffordshire, UK
c1892–1909

Robinson & Leadbeater
Stoke, Staffordshire, UK
1864–1924
This mark c1885–

Retsch & Co.
Wunsiedel, Bavaria, Germany
1885–

Rosenthal
Selb, Bavaria, Germany
1879–
This mark c1891–1904

Low, Ratcliffe & Co.
Longton, Staffordshire, UK
1882–92

Rauenstein
Thuringia, Germany
1783–1901

Pierre Roussencq
Marans-la-Rochelle,
Charente-Inférieure,
France
1740–50s

Robineau Pottery
Syracuse, NY, USA
c1905–28

Rookwood Pottery
Cincinnati, OH, USA
1880–1967

Reinhold Schlegelmilch
Tillowitz, Silesia, Germany
1869–

Alfred Voigt
Sitzendorf, Thuringia, Germany
1850–1977

Caughley/Salopian
Nr. Brosley, Shropshire, UK
c1750–99
This mark 1775–99

Gotha

Thuringia, Germany

1757–1937
This mark 1883–

Sebastian Schmidt

Schmiedefeld, Thuringia, Germany

1857–c1913

Sèvres

France

1756–

This mark for stoneware
1900–

This mark for porcelain
1900–

Union Porcelain

Greenpoint, Long Island, NY, USA

1863–c1922

Maximilien-Joseph Bettignies

Saint-Amand-les-Eaux, Nord, France

1818–80

Sampson Bridgwood & Son

Longton, Staffordshire, UK

c1805–

This mark c1853–

This mark 1885

Shore, Coggins & Holt

Longton, Staffordshire, UK

c1905–10

De Grieksche A Factory

Delft, Holland

1674–87

Paul Revere Pottery / Saturday Evening Girls

Boston, Brighton, MA, USA

1907–42

Steubenville Pottery Co.

Steubenville, OH, USA

1879–1959

Cafaggiolo
Nr. Florence, Tuscany,
Italy
1498–18thC

**Giuseppe Sinibaldi
& Lodovico Santini**
Trieste, Italy
1783–early 19thC

Sceaux
Seine, France
1749–
This mark c1763–

Carl Thieme
Potschappel, Dresden,
Germany
1872–

Tiffany Studios
Corona, NY, USA
1902–32

**Turner &
Tomkinson**
Tunstall, Staffordshire,
UK
1860–72

Thomas Cone Ltd.
Longton, Staffordshire,
UK
1892–
This mark 1912–35

Ruskin Pottery
Smethwick,
Nr. Birmingham, UK
1898–1935
*This mark for proprietor
W Howson Taylor*

Klösterle
Bohemia, Germany
c1797–
This mark c1895–

Elton Pottery
Stoke, Staffordshire, UK
1956–
*This mark for designer
Thomas Mayer 1956–60*

Thomas Morris
Longton, Staffordshire,
UK
c1897–1901

Mosaic Tile Co.
Zanesville, OH, USA
1894–1967

CERAMICS

Plymouth Porcelain
Devon, UK
1768–70
This mark for John Toulouse

Carl Thieme
Potschappel, Dresden, Germany
1872–
This mark c1901–

Trenton Potteries
Trenton, NJ, USA
1892–1960

Taylor, Smith & Taylor
East Liverpool, OH, USA
1901–72

Taylor, Tunnicliffe & Co.
Hanley, Staffordshire, UK
1868–
This mark c1875–98

Union Céramique
Limoges, Haute-Vienne, France
1900–

Union Porcelain
Greenpoint, Long Island, NY, USA
1863–c1922

Villegoureix Noël & Co.
Limoges, Haute-Vienne, France
1922–29

Jabez Vodrey
East Liverpool, OH, USA
1858–1928

New Milford Pottery Co. / Wannopee Pottery
New Milford, CT, USA
1886–1903 This mark 1890–1903

Wardle & Co. Ltd.
Hanley, Staffordshire, UK
1871–1935
This mark c1890–1935

Willets Manufacturing Co.
Trenton, NJ, USA
1879–1908

H M Williamson & Sons
Longton, Staffordshire, UK
c1879–1941

This mark c1903–

Wileman & Co.
Fenton and Longton, Staffordshire, UK
1892–1925

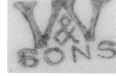

West End Pottery Co.
East Liverpool, OH, USA
1893–1938

James Macintyre
Burslem, Staffordshire, UK
1860–1928
This mark for designer William Moorcroft

Württembergische Metallwarenfabrik (WMF)
Geislingen, Germany
1853–

Wiener Werkstätte
Vienna, Austria
1903–32

Zurich
Switzerland
1765–90

Peters & Reed / Zane Pottery Co.
Zanesville, OH, USA
1898–1941
This mark 1921–

Adderley's Ltd.
Longton, Staffordshire, UK
1906–
This mark 1912–26

Alfred Meakin Ltd.
Tunstall, Staffordshire, UK
1875–

This mark c1875–97

This mark c1945–

Charles Allerton & Sons
Longton, Staffordshire, UK
1859–1942
This mark c1903–12

Oude Amstel
Holland
1784–c1800

Arabia
Helsinki, Finland
1874–

Arthur Bowker
Fenton, Staffordshire, UK
1950–58

William Ault
Nr. Burton-on-Trent,
Staffordshire, UK
1887–1923

John Aynsley & Sons
Longton, Staffordshire, UK
1864–

This mark c1891–1905

This mark 1934–39

Babbacombe Pottery Ltd.
Torquay, Devon, UK
1952–

Barker Bros. Ltd.
Longton, Staffordshire, UK
1876–
This mark 1937–

Ernest Batchelder
Los Angeles, CA, USA
1909–early 1950s
This mark 1912–32

Bay Keramik
Ransbach-Baumbach, West
Germany
1933–

Beauce Pottery
Beauce, QC, Canada
1939–89

Shore & Coggins
Longton, Staffordshire, UK
1911–66
This mark c1936–66

Belleek
Co Fermanagh, Northern Ireland, UK
1863–

This mark 1926–46

This mark 1946–55

Ford & Sons Ltd.
Burslem, Staffordshire, UK
c1894–1938
This mark 1908–

Royal Porcelain Factory Berlin
Berlin, Germany
1763–

This mark 1847–49

This mark 1849–70

Minton Hollins & Co.
Stoke-on-Trent, Staffordshire, UK
c1793–
This mark c1868

Bernard Moore
Stoke-on-Trent, Staffordshire, UK
1905–15

Beswick
Stoke-on-Trent, Staffordshire, UK
1892–

This mark 1955–72

This mark 1973–74

This mark 1998–2002

Bishop & Stonier Ltd.
Hanley, Staffordshire, UK
1891–1939
This mark c1936–39

Derby Porcelain
Derbyshire, UK
c1750–
This mark
c1820–40

Blue Mountain Pottery
Collingwood, ON, Canada
1947–2004

This label 1960s

This label 1967–72

This label 1976–2004

Names

CERAMICS

Booths Ltd.
Tunstall, Staffordshire, UK
c1891–1948

This mark c1891–1906

This mark 1912–

These marks c1930–

Branksome China
Fordingbridge, Hampshire, UK
1945–2009

Tooth & Co. Ltd.
Woodville, Derbyshire, UK
1883–1996

Briglin Pottery
London, UK
1947–90

Brown-Westhead, Moore & Co.
Hanley, Staffordshire, UK
1862–1904
This mark 1890–

Burgess & Leigh Ltd.
Burslem, Staffordshire, UK
1862–

This mark 1930s

*This mark 1939–
With 'Ironstone' 1960–*

150

Burmantofts
Leeds, Yorkshire, UK
1882–1904

H J Wood Ltd.
Burslem, Staffordshire, UK
1884–
This mark c1920s

Ida Perrin
Bushey Heath, London, UK
1921–33
This mark for decorator F Passenger

C H Brannam Ltd.
Barnstaple, Devon, UK
1879–2005
This mark 1913–

Candy & Co.
Devon, UK
1875–1998

Wiltshaw & Robinson Ltd.
Stoke-on-Trent, Staffordshire, UK
1890–1957
This mark c1894–

Carlton Ware Ltd.
Stoke-on-Trent, Staffordshire, UK
1958–92

This mark c1930–

This mark c1980–

Carn Pottery
Cornwall, UK
1971–

Cauldon Ltd.
Hanley, Staffordshire, UK
1905–20

Chamberlains & Co.
Worcester, UK
c1786–1852
This mark 1846–50

New Chelsea Porcelain Co. Ltd.
Longton, Staffordshire, UK
c1912–51 This mark c1913–

Linthorpe Pottery
Linthorpe, Middlesbrough, UK
c1879–89
This mark for designer Christopher Dresser (1834–1904)

Cinque Ports Pottery (Rye Art Pottery)
Rye, East Sussex, UK
1957–2006

Arthur J Wilkinson Ltd.
Burslem, Staffordshire, UK
1885–
This mark for designer Clarice Cliff c1930–

Clementson Bros. Ltd.
Hanley, Staffordshire, UK
c1839–1916
This mark 1913–16

CERAMICS

George Clews & Co.
Tunstall, Staffordshire, UK
1906–61

These marks 1935–

James & Ralph Clews
Cobridge, Staffordshire, UK
1818–34

Coalport Porcelain
Coalport, Shropshire and Stoke-on-Trent, Staffordshire, UK
c1795–

This mark c1805–15

This mark c1891–1939

Ridgway Potteries Ltd.
Stoke-on-Trent, Staffordshire, UK
1955–64

Honiton Art Potteries Ltd.
Honiton, Devon, UK
1918–47
This mark for proprietor C Collard

Copeland & Garrett
Stoke-on-Trent, Staffordshire, UK
c1833–47

W T Copeland & Sons Ltd.
Stoke-on-Trent, Staffordshire, UK
1847–

This mark c1891–1970

This mark 1906–

Parrott & Co. Ltd.
Burslem, Staffordshire, UK
c1921–60s
Mark with 'Made in England'
1935–

A G Richardson & Co. Ltd.
Tunstall, Staffordshire, UK
1915–82

This mark c1916–

This mark c1925–

This mark for designer
Charlotte Rhead c1930

Crown Staffordshire Porcelain Co. Ltd.
Fenton, Staffordshire, UK
1889–1973

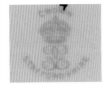

These marks 1906–

This mark 1930s–

A B & R P Daniell & Son
(retailers)
Wigmore Street, London, UK
c1825–1917

Davenport
Longport, Staffordshire, UK
c1793–1887

This mark c1815–30

This mark 1820–60

Dedham Pottery
Dedham, MA, USA
1896–1943
This mark 1896–1928

This mark c1805–20

**DAVENPORT
LONGPORT
STAFFORDSHRE**

This mark c1870–86

Joseph Bourne & Son Ltd.
Denby, Derbyshire, UK
1809–1970

This mark c1930–

This mark c1975–87

Giovanni De Simone
Palermo, Sicily, Italy
c1944–2008

Dihl & Guerhard
Paris, France
1781–c1824

Plateelbakkerij de Distel
Holland
1895–1923
Mark for Theodoor Nieuwenhuis

William De Morgan Pottery
Chelsea, Merton Abbey and
Fulham, London, UK
c1872–1907
*This mark for decorator Joe Juster,
Fulham, 1888–1907*

Doulton & Co. Ltd.
Lambeth, London, UK
c1854–1956
This mark c1880–1902

Donath & Co.
Dresden, Germany
1872–1916

Edwards & Brown
Longton, Staffordshire, UK
1882–1933
This mark 1910–33

Edward & George Phillips
Longport, Staffordshire, UK
1822–34

Empire Porcelain Co. Ltd.
Stoke-on-Trent, Staffordshire, UK
1896–1967
This mark 1930s

Enoch Wedgwood Ltd.
Tunstall, Staffordshire, UK
1860–1980
This mark 1965–

Francis Morley & Co.
Shelton, Hanley, Staffordshire, UK
1845–58

F T Thomas
(retailers)
Quebec, QB, Canada
Late 19thC

Marcello Fantoni
(1915–2011)
Italy
This mark 1950s–70s

Thomas Fell & Co. Ltd.
Newcastle upon Tyne, UK
c1817–90
This mark 1830–

G M & C J Mason
Fenton, Staffordshire, UK
1813–29
This mark 1825–29

S Fielding & Co. Ltd.
Stoke-on-Trent, Staffordshire, UK
1879–1982

This mark c1891–1913

This mark c1917–30

This mark c1930–

CERAMICS

Homer Laughlin China Co.
Newell, WV, USA
1936–73 and 1985–

J Fischer Ceramic Factory
Budapest, Hungary
c1895–1913

Worcester Porcelains
Worcester, UK
c1751–
This mark Flight c1783–92

Wileman & Co.
Fenton and Longman,
Staffordshire, UK
1892–1925

E Brain & Co. Ltd.
Fenton, Staffordshire, UK
1903–63
This mark 1948–63

Imported goods
c1891–1923
*This mark for imported goods
often from Japan*

Thomas Forester & Sons Ltd.
Longton, Staffordshire, UK
1883–1959
This mark 1912–59

**Fulper
Pottery**
Flemington,
NJ, USA
*1814–1935
This mark
c1922–28
After 1935 wares
were marked
'Stangl'*

George Clews & Co. Ltd.
Tunstall, Staffordshire, UK
1906–61
This mark 1935–

George Grainger & Co.
Worcester, UK
c1839–1902
This mark 1839–60

Winfield Pottery
Pasadena, CA, USA
1929–62
This mark 1939–62

Gardner Porcelain
Nr. Moscow, Russia
c1765–1891
This mark late 19thC

Schmidt & Co.
Czechoslovakia
1883–1945
This mark 1918–45

George Jones & Sons Ltd.
Stoke-on-Trent, Staffordshire, UK
c1864–1957

This mark c1901–21

This mark c1924–51

Glidden Pottery
Alfred, NY, USA
1940–57

Goebel Porcelain
Oeslau-Rödental, Nr. Coburg, Germany
1871–
This mark 1972–79

CERAMICS

Goldscheider Porcelain
Vienna, Austria
1885–1963

This mark c1922–41

This label 1922–42

A B Jones & Sons Ltd.
Longton, Staffordshire, UK
1900–72
This mark 1935–

A E Gray & Co. Ltd.
Hanley and Stoke-on-Trent, Staffordshire, UK
c1912–61

This mark 1930–33

This mark 1934–

W H Grindley & Co Ltd.
Tunstall, Staffordshire, UK
c1880–1960
This mark c1936–54

Grueby Faience Co.
Boston, MA, USA
1894–1920

Gustavsberg Porcelain
Nr. Stockholm, Sweden
1827–

*This mark for designer Stig
Lindberg 1937–80*

Argenta series 1930–50s

Hackwood & Keeling
Hanley, Staffordshire, UK
1835–36

James Hadley & Sons Ltd.
Worcester, UK
1896–1905
This mark 1897–1902

Haeger Potteries Inc.
Dundee, IL, USA
1874–
This mark 1914–

Hammersley & Co.
Longton, Staffordshire, UK
1887–1982
This mark 1939–

H M Williamson & Sons
Longton, Staffordshire, UK
c1879–1941
This mark c1928–41

Henriot Quimper
Brittany, France
1690–
This mark c1922–

Herculaneum Pottery
Liverpool, UK
1796–1841
This mark c1796–1833

Herend Porcelain
Nr. Veszprém, Hungary
1826–

This mark 1935–38

This mark 1976–

TRADE MARK
HOBSON
B

George Hobson
Burslem, Staffordshire, UK
1901–23

G & J Hobson
Burslem, Staffordshire, UK
1883–1901

**Hornsea Pottery
Co. Ltd.**
Hornsea, Yorkshire, UK
*c1950–2000
This mark 1960–*

Thomas Hughes & Son Ltd.
Burslem, Staffordshire, UK
*1895–1957
This mark 1935–57*

Hutschenreuther Porcelain
Selb, Bavaria, Germany
c1856–

Iden Pottery
Rye, East Sussex, UK
1961–2002

International Art Ware Corporation (Inarco)
Cleveland, OH, USA
1960–86

Irving W Rice & Co.
New York, NY, USA
1920s–
Major importers

Iroquois China Co.
Syracuse, NY, USA
1905–67
This mark for Russel Wright
1947–67

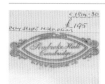

John & William Ridgway
Hanley, Staffordshire, UK
c1814–30

**Jean Cocteau
(1889–1963)**
France
This mark 1957–63

John Hall & Sons
Burslem, Staffordshire, UK
1814–32

**Jean Lurçat
(1892–1966)**
St Vincens, Perpignan, France
This mark 1950–66

James Kent Ltd.
Longton, Staffordshire, UK
1897–

This mark c1950   *These marks 1955–*

James Macintyre & Co.
Burslem, Staffordshire, UK
c1860–1928

This mark c1896–98

This mark for designer William Moorcroft 1897–1912

Jérôme Massier Fils
Vallauris, France
This mark for Jean Baptiste Massier c1870–1910

John Maddock & Sons Ltd.
Burslem, Staffordshire, UK
1855–1960s

This mark c1896–

This mark c1945–

Johnson Bros. (Hanley) Ltd.
Hanley, Staffordshire, UK
1883–2004

These marks c1913–

Friedrich Kaestner
Oberhohndorf, Nr. Zwickau, Germany
1883–

Keele Street Pottery Co. Ltd.
Tunstall and Longton, Staffordshire, UK
1915–
This mark 1962–

Keeling & Co. Ltd.
Burslem, Staffordshire, UK
1886–1936
This mark c1912–36

Boch Frères
Saint-Vaast, Belgium
1844–

This mark 1891–

*This mark for designer Charles
Catteau c1922–30*

Krautheim Porcelain
Selb, Bavaria, Germany
1912–78

Kronach Porcelain
Upper Franconia, Germany
1897–

Lancaster & Sandland Ltd.
Hanley, Staffordshire, UK
1949–68

Alexander Lauder
Barnstaple, Devon, UK
1876–1914

Leeds Pottery
Yorkshire, UK
c1758–1820   This mark c1781–1820

Lenci Ceramics
Turin, Italy
1928–64

Lladró Porcelain
Almácera, Nr. Valencia, Spain
c1953–

Locke & Co.
Worcester, UK
1896–1914
This mark c1898–1902

Lorna Bailey
(b. 1978)
Stoke-on-Trent, Staffordshire, UK
Active 1995–2008

Louis Wain
(1860–1939)
London, UK
This mark c1914

Lovatt & Lovatt
Nr. Nottingham, UK
1895–

James Macintyre & Co.
Burslem, Staffordshire, UK
c1860–1928
This mark c1891–1900

Mackin & Potts
Burslem, Staffordshire, UK
1833–37

Made in Occupied Japan
1945–52

C T Maling & Sons Ltd.
Newcastle upon Tyne, Northumberland, UK
1762–1963

This mark 1924–58

This mark c1958–63

Royal Copenhagen
Denmark
1775–
This mark for designer
Nils Thorsson 1950s

Price Bros. (Burslem) Ltd.
Burslem, Staffordshire, UK
1896–1961
This mark c1930s–

J W McCoy Pottery
Roseville and Zanesville,
OH, USA
1910–91

G M & C J Mason
Lane Delph,
Staffordshire, UK
1813–29

This mark c1813–25

This mark c1813–25

This mark c1820

McCarty's Pottery
Merigold, MS, USA
1954–

J & G Meakin Ltd.
Hanley, Staffordshire, UK
1851–2000
This mark 1953–

Ernst Teichert
Meissen, Saxony,
Germany
1884–c1940
Not to be confused
with the Meissen
factory, which
never used the word
'Meissen' on wares

Mettlach Pottery
Saar Basin, Germany
1809–
This mark late 19thC

W R Midwinter Ltd.
Burslem, Staffordshire, UK
c1910–87

This mark 1932–41

This mark c1946–

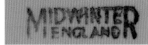

This mark 1960s

This mark 1970–87

Minton
Stoke-on-Trent, Staffordshire, UK
c1793–

This mark 1863–72

Mark used c1862–71
This mark 1867

This mark c1873–91   *This mark c1891–1902*

This mark
c1891–1910

This mark 1951–

Mitterteich
Bavaria, Germany
1916–2006

W Moorcroft Ltd.
Burslem, Staffordshire, UK
1913–

This mark 1928–49

This mark 1986–

Moore Bros.
Longton, Staffordshire, UK
1872–1905
This mark 1902–05

Sampson & Hancock & Sons
Stoke-on-Trent,
Staffordshire, UK
c1857–1937
*This mark for designer
George Cartlidge 1912–37*

Mortlock's
(retailers)
Oxford Street, London, UK
1746–c1930

C G Schierholz & Söhn
Plaue, Thuringia, Germany
c1816–
'Musterschutz' means copyrighted or patent protected

169

This mark c1936–
The 'BAG' mark indicates items
made for export by British
American Glass

Myott, Son & Co. Ltd.
Stoke-on-Trent, Cobridge and
Hanley, Staffordshire, UK
1898–1976

This mark c1930–

This mark c1936–

This mark c1959–

Natzler Pottery
Los Angeles, CA, USA
1937–71

New Hall Pottery Co. Ltd.
Hanley, Staffordshire, UK
1899–1956
This mark c1930–51

Noritake
Nish-ku, Nagoya, Japan
1904–

This mark 1911–41

This mark 1933–40

NYMÖLLE
DENMARK
Artist:
3118-700

Nymølle
Denmark
1946–90s
This mark for designer B Wiinblad

Nymphenburg Porcelain
Neudeck ob der Au,
Munich, Germany
1747–
This mark 20thC

Sampson Smith Ltd.
Longton, Staffordshire, UK
c1845–1963
This mark c1930–41

Ott & Brewer
Trenton, NJ, USA
1863–93
This mark 1885

P L Dagoty
Paris, France
1804–

Star China Co.
Longton, Staffordshire, UK
1900–1919
This mark c1913–

Paragon China Co. Ltd.
Longton, Staffordshire, UK
1920–64

This mark c1932–

This mark c1939–49

This mark c1952–

Madoura
Vallauris,
France
*This mark
for designer
Pablo Picasso
1947–71*

Pinxton
Derbyshire, UK
c1796–1813

Poole Pottery
Carter, Stabler & Adams Ltd.
1921–

This mark 1921–

This mark 1921–

This mark 1956–

This mark c1960

This mark 1963–

Portmeirion Potteries Ltd.
Stoke-on-Trent, Staffordshire, UK
1962–

This mark 1962–

This mark 1962–

This mark 1972–

H J Wood Ltd.

Burslem, Staffordshire, UK

1884–

This mark 1920s

Samuel Radford Ltd.

Fenton, Staffordshire, UK

1879–1957

This mark c1880–91

Pountney & Co. Ltd.

Bristol, Avon, UK

c1816–

This mark 1939–

Rambervillers Pottery

Vosges, France

1903–40

This mark for designer A Cytère

Red Wing Pottery

Red Wing, MN, USA

1877–1967

Reid & Co.

Longton, Staffordshire, UK

1913–46

This mark 1913–

Richard Ginori

Milan, Italy

1735–2011

This mark mid 20thC

Ridgway (Bedford Works)

Hanley, Staffordshire, UK

1920–52

This mark c1950–52

Also used by Ridgway Potteries

Ltd. 1955–64

Ridgway Potteries Ltd.

Stoke-on-Trent, Staffordshire, UK

1955–64

This mark c1962–

Rockingham
Swinton, Yorkshire, UK
c1745–1842

This mark c1826–30

This mark c1830–42

This mark 1842–

Rörstrand
Stockholm & Gothenburg, Sweden
1726–2005
This mark 1950s

Rosenthal Porcelain
Selb, Bavaria, Germany
1891–

This mark 1919–35

This mark 1922–

Roseville Pottery
Roseville, OH, USA
1890–1954

This label c1927–35

This mark 1936–40

This mark c1940–53

Thomas C Wild & Sons Ltd.
Longton, Staffordshire, UK
1917–

Rowland & Marcellus & Co.
(Importers, wholesalers, retailers)
New York, NY, USA
c1893–1938

This mark c1917–35

This mark 1945–

*Royal Albert
Ltd.1970–
This mark 1989–98*

Royal Bayreuth
Tettau, Franconia, Germany
*1794–
This mark 1891–*

New Chelsea China
Co. Ltd.
Longton, Staffordshire, UK
1936–61

George Grainger & Co.
Worcester, UK
*c1839–1902
Mark used c1889–1902
This mark with date letter
for 1902*

Royal Copenhagen
Denmark
*1775–
This mark 1969–74*

Royal Crown
Derby
Derbyshire, UK
*1876–
This mark c1891–
c1920*

175

CERAMICS

Royal Doulton
Lambeth, London, UK
c1858–
This mark c1902–30

A B Jones & Sons Ltd.
Longton, Staffordshire, UK
1900–72
This mark 1957–72

**Pilkington's Tile
& Pottery Co. Ltd.**
Nr. Manchester, Lancashire, UK
c1897–1938 and 1948–57

This mark c1914–38

This mark c1920–38

Royal Stafford China
Longton, Staffordshire, UK
1952–

Arthur J Wilkinson Ltd.
Burslem, Staffordshire, UK
1885–
This mark 1930s–

Chapmans Longton Ltd.
Longton, Staffordshire, UK
1916–

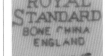

This mark 1930–49

This mark 1949–

R H & S L Plant Ltd.
Longton, Staffordshire, UK
1898–
This mark 1967–

Grimwades Ltd.
Stoke-on-Trent, Staffordshire, UK
1900–

This mark c1934–50

This mark c1951–

Worcester Porcelains
Worcester, UK
c1751–
Mark used 1891–
This mark 1906

Roseville Pottery
Roseville, OH, USA
1890–1954
Rozane ware 1905–23

Rozenburg
The Hague, Holland
c1883–1915
This mark 1902

Ruskin Pottery
Smethwick, Nr. Birmingham, UK
1898–1935

This mark 1904–
Mark with 'Made in England'
1920–

Mark used 1904–15 This mark 1906

Rye Pottery
Rye, East Sussex, UK
1869–

This mark 1955–56

This mark 1957–

James Sadler & Sons Ltd.
Burslem, Staffordshire, UK
c1899–
This mark c1947–

Carl Schumann
Arzberg, Bavaria, Germany
1881–1994
This mark 1926–

Shelley Potteries Ltd.
Longton, Staffordshire, UK
1925–66

This mark 1925–40

This mark c1944–66

Shorter & Son Ltd.
Stoke-on-Trent, Staffordshire, UK
1900–64
This mark 1940–64

Simpsons Potters Ltd.
Cobridge, Staffordshire, UK
1944–2004

Josiah Spode
Stoke-on-Trent, Staffordshire, UK
c1784–1833

This mark c1790–1805

This mark c1790–1820

This mark c1805–15

This mark c1805–33

This mark c1815–30

Star Pottery
Posail Park, Glasgow, Scotland, UK
1880–1907

Stavangerflint
Stavanger, Norway
1949–79
This mark 1952–79

Steubenville Pottery
Steubenville, OH, USA
1879–1959
This mark 1939–59

Stonier & Co.
(retailer)
Liverpool, UK
1910–33
This mark c1905

Names

CERAMICS

Susie Cooper
Burslem, Staffordshire, UK
c1930–

This mark 1930–31

This mark 1932–56

This mark 1932–64

Shaw & Copestake
Longton, Staffordshire, UK
1901–82

This mark 1940s–50s

This mark for export pieces 1930s

This mark 1946–50s

This mark 1950s

This mark 1960s–82

T G Green & Co. Ltd.
Church Gresley, Derbyshire, UK
c1864–

This mark 1930s–

This mark 20thC

This mark 1930s–

This mark 1970s–

Thomas Goode & Co.
(retailer)
Mayfair, London, UK
This mark late 19thC–c1920s

Thomas, John & Joseph Mayer
Burslem, Staffordshire, UK
1843–55

Troika Pottery
St Ives and Newlyn, Cornwall, UK
1963–83

Toni Raymond Pottery
Torquay, Devon, UK
1951–86

This mark 1960s

This mark 1960s

*This mark for decorator
Alison Brigden 1977–83*

*This mark for decorator
Avril Bennett 1973–79*

*This mark for decorator
Benny Sirota 1963–80*

*This mark for decorator
Honor Curtis 1969–73, 1975*

*This mark for decorator
Marilyn Pascoe late 1960s–74*

*This mark for decorator
Shirley Warf 1979–81*

Names

CERAMICS

Turner & Co.
Longton, Staffordshire, UK
c1763–1806
This mark c1800–05

R H & S L Plant Ltd.
Longton, Staffordshire, UK
1898–
This mark 1947–53

Unterweissbach
Thuringia, Germany
1958–76

Van Briggle Pottery
Colorado Springs, CO, USA
1901–

Vienna (Franz Dörfl)
Austria
c1880–c1925

Vienna
Augarten, Austria
1922–

Elektra Porcelain Co. Ltd.
Longton, Staffordshire, UK
1924–c1975
This mark 1940s–

William De Morgan Pottery

Chelsea, Merton Abbey and Fulham, London, UK

c1872–1907

This mark c1882–
With '& Co.' 1888–

This mark c1888–

This mark c1888–

William Henry Goss Ltd.
Stoke-on-Trent, Staffordshire, UK
1862–1944
This mark c1862–91

William Ridgway & Co.
Hanley, Staffordshire, UK
1830–54
This mark 1835

Wade, Heath & Co. Ltd.
Burslem, Staffordshire, UK
1927–

Washington Pottery Ltd.
Shelton, Staffordshire, UK
1946–73

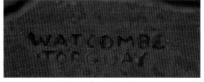

Watcombe Pottery Co.
Torquay, Devon, UK
1867–1901
This mark 1867–75

Names

J H Weatherby & Sons Ltd.
Hanley, Staffordshire, UK
1891–2000

This mark 1930s

This mark 1936

Wedgwood & Bentley
Longton, Staffordshire, UK
c1769–80

Josiah Wedgwood & Sons Ltd.
Tunstall, Staffordshire, UK
c1759–2009

This mark c1759–69

This mark c1920–

Weller Pottery
Fultonham and Zanesville, OH, USA
1872–1948

This mark c1900–25

This mark 1930s

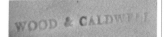

Wood & Caldwell
Burslem, Staffordshire, UK
c1790–1818

Worcester Porcelains
Worcester, UK
c1751–
This mark 1750s RH for Robert Hancock, engraver
and designer, and anchor for Richard Holdship

Worcester Porcelains
Worcester, UK
c1751–
This mark Barr, Flight & Barr
c1807–13
Written marks, such as this,
are usually found on the best
examples of the factory's
output

**Worcester
Porcelains**
Worcester, UK
c1751–
This mark Flight, Barr
& Barr
c1813–40

Zsolnay Pecs
Hungary
c1863–91

Swords

Meissen
Nr. Dresden, Saxony, Germany
1710–

This mark 1763–74

*This mark for Marcolini period
c1774–1814*

This mark 1814–

This mark 19thC–c1925

*This mark for Pfeiffer
period 1924–34*

This mark early 20thC–

Champion's Bristol
Bristol, Avon, UK
c1770–81

Coalport Porcelain
Coalport, Shropshire, UK
c1795–
This mark c1810–25

Derby Porcelain
Derbyshire, UK
c1750–
This mark c1780–1830

Carl Thieme
Potschappel, Dresden,
Germany
1872–

Fontainebleau
Seine-et-Marne, France
1795–
*This mark for proprietor
Jacob Petit 1862–65*

Locré & Russinger
La Courtille, Paris, France
c1773–1820
This mark c1773–c1820

Longton Hall
Staffordshire, UK
c1749–60

Lowestoft
Suffolk, UK
1757–c1802
This mark 1775–90

Nymphenburg
Bavaria, Germany
1747–
This mark for Turkish market mid 1760s

Ruskin Pottery
Smethwick,
Nr. Birmingham, UK
1898–1935
This mark 1913

Tournai
Belgium
1751–1850
This mark 1756–81

Volkstedt
Rudolstadt, Thuringia, Germany
1760–

These marks after 1787–

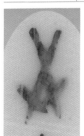

Wallendorf
Thuringia, Germany
1763–1833
This mark before 1780

Weesp
Holland
1764–71

Worcester Porcelains
Worcester, UK
c1751–
This mark c1760–70

Crowns

Bock-Wallendorf
Thuringia, Germany
1903–90

Chesapeake Pottery / D F Haynes & Son
Baltimore, MD, USA
1880–1924

Crown Pottery Co.
Evansville, IN, USA
1891–1955

Derby Porcelain
Derbyshire, UK
c1750–

This mark 1806–25

This mark c1878–90

Frankenthal
Palatinate, Germany
1755–99
*This mark for Carl
Theodor 1762–88*

Goebel Porcelain
Nr. Coburg, Germany
1871–

Grimwades Ltd.
Stoke-on-Trent,
Staffordshire, UK
1900–

Höchst
Nr. Mainz, Germany
1746–
This mark c1765–74

Ludwigsburg
Württemberg, Germany
1758–1824
This mark 1758–93

C G Schierholz & Söhn
Plaue, Thuringia, Germany
1816–

Sèvres
France
1756–

This mark for pâte dure (hard paste) 1769–93   *This mark c1845–48*

Volkstedt
Rudolstadt, Thuringia, Germany
1760–
This mark is modern

Worcester Porcelains
Worcester, UK
Mark for Worcester Royal Porcelain 1862–75
This mark often has the last two digits of the year underneath, e.g. '73' denotes 1873

St Petersburg
Russia
1744–1917

This mark for Catherine II 1796–1801

This mark for Alexander II c1855–71

This mark for Nicholas II 1894–1917

Stars & Crosses

Royal Porcelain Factory Berlin
Berlin, Germany
1763–
This mark for WWI 1914–18

Champion's Bristol
Bristol, Avon, UK
c1770–81

Florence (possibly workshop of Giunta di Tugio)
Tuscany, Italy
This mark 1425–50

Fulda
Hesse, Germany
1741–89
This mark c1765–80

Ginori Factory
Doccia, Tuscany, Italy
1735–
These marks late 18th/early 19thC

Lowestoft
Suffolk, UK
1757–c1802

Nymphenburg
Bavaria, Germany
1747–
This mark 1763–67

Animals

Saint-Cloud
Seine-et-Oise, France
1693–1766

Girolamo Salomone
Savona, Liguria, Italy
17th/18thC

Samson-Edmé et Cie.
Paris, France
1845–1969

Samuel Barker & Son
Swinton, Yorkshire, UK
1834–93
This mark 1851–

Chelsea Keramic Art Works / Dedham Pottery
Chelsea, MA, USA
1872–1943

Fürstenberg
Brunswick, Germany
c1753–
This mark used on busts late 18thC

Frankenthal
Palatinate, Germany
c1756–59

The Hague
Holland
1775–90

Kassel
Hesse-Nassau, Germany
1766–1862

This mark for earthenware 1771–1862

This mark for porcelain 1786–88

CERAMICS

Lille
France
1784–1817

**New England
Pottery Co.**
East Boston, MA, USA
1854–1914

Nyon
Nr. Geneva, Switzerland
1781–1813

Onondaga Pottery
Syracuse, NY, USA
1871–1966

**Paul Revere
Pottery /
Saturday
Evening
Girls**
Boston and
Brighton, MA,
USA
1907–42

Shields

Ansbach
Bavaria, Germany
c1708–
This mark for faience

**Carl Magnus
Hutschenreuther**
Bavaria, Germany
1814–
This mark c1865-

Nymphenburg
Bavaria, Germany
1747–
This mark mid 19thC

Vienna
Austria
1718–1864
This mark from 1784–

CERAMICS

Anchors

Anchor Porcelain Co. Ltd.

Longton, Staffordshire, UK

1901–18

This mark 1901–15

Chelsea Porcelain Works

London, UK

c1745–69

This mark 1752–56

This mark c1756–69

Geminiano Cozzi

Venice, Italy

1765–

Derby Porcelain

Derbyshire, UK

1750–

These marks 1769–75

Thomas Fell & Co. Ltd.

Newcastle upon Tyne, UK

c1817–90

This mark 1817–30

Thomas Furnival & Sons

Cobridge, Staffordshire, UK

18thC – 1968

This mark 1878–

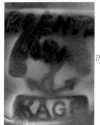

Gustavsberg

Nr. Stockholm, Sweden

1827–

This mark for designer Wilhelm Kage 1917–

Poppelsdorf (Ludwig Wessel)

Rhineland, Germany

1755–1829

Sceaux (Duc de Penthièvre)

Seine, France

c1735–

This mark c1775

CERAMICS

Circles

Höchst
Nr. Mainz, Germany
1746–
This mark 1763–96

Rookwood
Cincinnati, OH,
USA
1880–1967
*This mark
c1886–*

Josiah Spode
Stoke, Staffordshire, UK
c1784–1833
This mark c1790–1820

**Worcester
Porcelains**
Worcester, UK
c1751–
This mark 1852–62

Crescents

**Oeslau &
Wilhelmsfeld
Porcelain Factory**
Oeslau, Bavaria,
Germany
1871–
*Taken over by
W Goebel 1879–*

Hanau
Frankfurt-am-Main,
Germany
1661–1806

Lowestoft
Lowestoft, Suffolk, UK
1757–c1802
This mark c1775–90

Pinxton
Derbyshire, UK
c1796–1813
This mark c1799–1806

Worcester Porcelains
Worcester, UK
c1751–

This mark c1755–90

This mark c1770–75

CERAMICS

Fleur-de-lys

Buen Retiro
Madrid, Spain
1759–
This mark 1760–1804

Capodimonte
Italy
1743–59

These marks c1745–59

Limoges
Haute-Vienne, France
1771–96
This mark 1784–96

Saint-Cloud
Seine-et-Oise, France
1693–1766
This mark c1700–66

Plants

De Roos
Delft, Holland
1662–1779
This mark early 18thC

J Glatz
Villingen, Baden,
Germany
1870–

**New England
Pottery Co.**
East Boston, MA, USA
1854–1914
This mark 1886–88

Minton Hollins & Co.
Stoke-on-Trent, Staffordshire, UK
1793–
This mark c1868

Shaw & Copestake
Longton, Staffordshire,
UK
1901–82
This mark c1925–36

CERAMICS

Scrolls

Thomas Dimmock Jnr. & Co.
Shelton and Hanley,
Staffordshire, UK
1828–59

De Porceleyne Klaeuw
Delft, Holland
1662–
This mark registered 1757

Ludwigsburg
Württemberg, Germany
1758–1824
This mark 1758–93

Samson-Edmé et Cie.
Paris, France
1845–1969

Vincennes
Paris, France
1740–56
This mark 1753

Triangles

Chelsea Porcelain Works
London, UK
c1745–69
This mark c1745–49

Goebel Porcelain
Nr. Coburg, Germany
1871–

This mark 1950–55

This mark 1960–63

Other Devices

William Ault
Nr. Burton-on-Trent,
Staffordshire, UK
1887–1923

Royal Porcelain Factory Berlin
Berlin, Germany
1763–
This mark 1820–37

Chantilly
Oise, France
1725–1800
This mark c1725–89

Other Devices

Clignancourt
Paris, France
1771–c1798

Royal Copenhagen
Denmark
1775–

This mark 1775

This mark 1830–45

This mark c1885

Red Wing Pottery Stoneware
Redwing, MN, USA
1877–1967

Samson-Edmé et Cie.
Paris, France
1845–1969

Ernst Teichert
Meissen, Saxony, Germany
1884–c1940
Not to be confused with the Meissen factory, which never used the word 'Meissen' on wares

Tournai
Belgium
1751–1850
This mark 1751–96

Worcester Porcelains
Worcester, UK
c1751–

Workman's mark c1751–65

This mark c1755–75

Some Important Studio Potters

Michael Cardew (1901–83)
Established Vume Pottery, Ghana 1945

Personal seal mark, Winchcombe, Gloucestershire and Wenford Bridge, Cornwall, UK

This mark Winchcombe c1926–39

This mark Wenford Bridge 1939–42

Hans Coper (1920–81)
Worked with Lucie Rie in London
1946–58
Hammersmith, London, then Digswell House, Herefordshire, UK
1958–67
Frome, Somerset, UK
1967–80

Bernard Leach (1887–1979)
St Ives, Cornwall, UK
'The Father of British studio pottery'

David Leach (1911–2005)
Bovey Tracey, Devon, UK

This mark for Lowerdown Pottery 1954–

John Maltby (b.1936)
Crediton, Devon, UK

CERAMICS

Martin Brothers
Fulham and Southall, London, UK
1873–1914

This mark 1874

This mark 1893

**George Ohr
(1857–1918)**
Biloxi, MS, USA

**Katherine
Pleydell-Bouverie
(1895–1985)**
Coleshill, Berkshire, UK

**Lucie Rie
(1902–95)**
London, UK

**Bernard Rooke
(b.1938)**
London and Swilland,
Suffolk, UK

**Edwin Scheier (1910–2008)
with Mary Scheier (1908–2007)**
Oaxaca, Mexico and Green Valley, AZ, USA

**William Staite
Murray
(1881–1962)**
Rotherhithe, London, UK

DESIGN REGISTRATION MARKS

One of the most useful marks for dating is the Design Registration mark. Registration began in 1839 following the Copyright of Design Act. The insignia (diamond-shaped mark) was used from 1842. The insignia also showed what material the item was made from (its class) and how many items were included (bundle or package). The Rd in the centre of the diamond stands for registered design.

	1842–67	1868–83
A	Class	Class
B	Year	Day
C	Month	Bundle
D	Day	Year
E	Bundle	Month

The exceptions to the following rules are: in 1857 the letter R was used 1–19 September in place of D; in 1860 the letter K was used during December in place of A. In both cases the clerks had forgotten to change the letter from the previous month. During 1–6 March 1878, W was used for the year in place of D, and G was used for the month in place of W.

Year

The letters were not used in sequence but as follows: 1842–67 (features a number in the right-hand corner of the diamond)

A	1845	F	1847	K	1857	P	1851	U	1848	Z	1860
B	1858	G	1863	L	1856	Q	1866	V	1850		
C	1844	H	1843	M	1859	R	1861	W	1865		
D	1852	I	1846	N	1864	S	1849	X	1842		
E	1855	J	1854	O	1862	T	1867	Y	1853		

1868–83 (letter in the right-hand corner of the diamond)

A	1871	E	1881	I	1872	L	1882	U	1874	Y	1879
C	1870	F	1873	J	1880	P	1877	V	1876		
D	1878	H	1869	K	1883	S	1875	X	1868		

Months

The months from both periods are shown as follows:

A	December	D	September	H	April	M	June
B	October	E	May	I	July	R	August
C/O	January	G	February	K	November	W	March

Class

Sometimes the clerks misclassified items so it is possible to find a bookbinding misfiled as a carpet.

Class 1	Metal	Class 7	Printed Shawls	Class 12 (i)	Other Fabrics
Class 2	Wood	Class 8	Other Shawls	Class 12 (ii)	Other Fabrics
Class 3	Glass	Class 9	Yarn		(Damasks)
Class 4	Earthenware	Class 10	Printed Fabrics	Class 13	Lace
Class 5	Paper Hangings	Class 11	Furnitures (printed		
Class 6	Carpets		fabrics)		

Registered Number

A series of consecutive numbers were used from 1884, nearly always prefixed by Rd or Rd No (Registered or Registered Number). This guide is an estimate only:

1	1884	205,240	1893	385,500	1902	751,160	1930
19,754	1885	224,720	1894	402,500	1903	837,520	1940
40,480	1886	246,975	1895	420,000	1904	860,854	1950
64,520	1887	268,393	1896	447,000	1905	895,000	1960
90,483	1888	291,241	1897	471,000	1906	944,932	1970
116,648	1889	311,658	1898	494,000	1907	993,012	1980
141,273	1890	331,707	1899	519,000	1908	2,007,720	1990
163,767	1891	351,202	1900	550,000	1909	2,089,190	2000
185,713	1892	368,154	1901	673,750	1920		

The system is still in use today.

CERAMICS

DERBY DATING CODES

From 1882, Derby Porcelain has used year cyphers.

 This mark was used c1878–90. At the time the company was known as the Derby Crown Porcelain Co. Ltd.

 Used from 1890 when the company name changed to Royal Crown Derby Porcelain Co. Ltd., this mark also includes the word 'England' from 1891, and 'Made in England' from c1920.

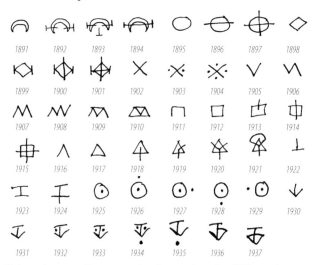

Derby continues to use Roman numerals to denote each year from 1938 onwards.

MINTON DATING CODES

From 1842, Minton has used impressed year cyphers. These are found in sets of three with the year cypher accompanied by a month letter and potter's mark.

Key to Month Letters:

J	January	M	March	E	May	H	July	S	September	N	November
F	February	A	April	I	June	Y	August	O	October	D	December

1842	1843	1844	1845	1846	1847	1848	1849	1850	1851
1852	1853	1854	1855	1856	1857	1858	1859	1860	1861
1862	1863	1864	1865	1866	1867	1868	1869	1870	1871
1872	1873	1874	1875	1876	1877	1878	1879	1880	1881
1882	1883	1884	1885	1886	1887	1888	1889	1890	1891
1892	1893	1894	1895	1896	1897	1898	1899	1900	1901
1902	1903	1904	1905	1906	1907	1908	1909	1910	1911
1912	1913	1914	1915	1916	1917	1918	1919	1920	1921
1922	1923	1924	1925	1926	1927	1928	1929	1930	1931
1932	1933	1934	1935	1936	1937	1938	1939	1940	1941	1942

This system was discontinued in 1943. Subsequently Minton used a numerical system where the last two digits denoted the year and preceding digits denoted the maker.

CERAMICS

NEWCOMB COLLEGE

Marks of decorators at Newcomb
Dates refer to years active at Newcomb

A A **Aurelia Coralie Arbo**
1931–40

AFS **Anna Frances Simpson**
1908–23, 1924–29

Amelie Roman
Faculty 1900–39

C.F. **Carmen Freret Favrot**
1918–29

CL **Cynthia Pugh Littlejohn**
1908–10, 1914–20

C.L. **Corinna Morgiana Luria**
1915–16

cmc **Corinne Marie Chalaron**
cMc *1922–24, 1925–26*

EFL **Emily Frances Lines**
1920–22

ES **Erin E Shepard**
1910–13

F5 **Anna Frances Simpson**
1908–23, 1924–29

JL **Julia (Hoerner) Michel**
1914–18

HB **Henrietta Davidson Bailey**
BH *1909–14, 1915–16*
Faculty 1926–38

J. M. **Juanita Maire Mauras**
1908–29

GF. **Emily Frances Lines**
1920–22

N **Leona Fischer Nicholson**
1908–09, 1913–14, 1922–26

MD **Marie Odell Delavigne**
M.D. *1908–25*

MGS **Mary Given Sheerer**
Faculty 1894–31

M-LB **Marie De Hoa LeBlanc**
MHL *1908–14*

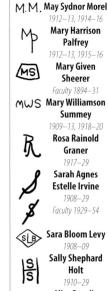

M.M. **May Sydnor Morel**
1912–13, 1914–16

MP **Mary Harrison Palfrey**
1912–13, 1915–16

MS **Mary Given Sheerer**
Faculty 1894–31

mWS **Mary Williamson Summey**
1909–13, 1918–20

R **Rosa Rainold Graner**
1917–29

S **Sarah Agnes Estelle Irvine**
1908–29
Faculty 1929–54

SLB **Sara Bloom Levy**
1908–09

S/S **Sally Shephard Holt**
1910–29

R **Alice Rosalie Urquhart**
1908–15, 1916–17

ROOKWOOD

The flame mark with Rookwood monogram was used from 1886 with an extra flame added each year – by 1900 there were 14 flames. In 1901 the Roman numeral I was added below the monogram and flames and changed accordingly with each year.

Marks of decorators at Rookwood
Dates refer to years active at Rookwood

AB	**Alfred L Brennan** *1881–84*	
A.D.S.	**Adeliza Drake Sehon** *1898–1902*	
A.F.	**Rose Fechheimer** *1896–1906*	
AG	**Arthur Goetting** *1896*	
A.H.	**Albert Humphreys/ Humphries** *1882–84*	
A.M.B.	**Anna M Bookprinter (later Valentien)** *1884–1905*	
AMV	**Anna M Valentien (née Bookprinter)** *1884–1905*	
AP	**Albert F Pons (Ponds)** *1904–11*	
A.R.V.	**Albert Robert Valentien** *1881–1905*	
AS	**Amelia B Sprague** *1887–1903*	
A.V.B	**Artus Van Briggle** *1886–99*	
B–	**Robert Bruce Horsfall** *1893–95*	
C	**Arthur P Conant** *1915–late 1920s*	
C.A.B.	**Constance A Baker** *1892–1904*	
CAD	**Cecil A Duell** *1907–17*	
CC	**Cora Crofton** *1886–92*	
C.C.L.	**Clara Christiana Lindeman** *1898–1909*	
C.F.B.	**Carolina F Bonsall** *1903–05*	
C.J.D.	**Charles John Dibowski** *1892–93*	
cJM	**Charles Jasper McLaughlin** *1913–20*	
C.N.	**Clara Chipman Newton** *1881–84*	
CNcn		
©	**Carl (Charles) Schmidt** *1896–1927*	
CS	**Caroline (Carrie) F Steinle** *1892–1925*	
C.S.T.	**Charles S Todd** *1911–20s*	

CERAMICS

CY	Grace Young *1886–1904*	
D.C.	Daniel Cook *1893–94*	
E.A.	Edward Abel *1890–92*	
E.B.I.C.	E Bertha I Cranch *1887*	
ELC	Eliza C Lawrence *1900–03*	
ED	Edward G Diers *1896–1931*	
E.D.F.	Emma D Foertmeyer *1887–92*	
EFM	Elizabeth F McDermott *1912–15*	
ELW	Edith L Wildman *1911–13*	
E.N.	Edith Noonan *1904–10*	
EPC	Edward P Cranch *1884–90*	
ERF.	Edith Felton *1896–1904*	
E.T.H.	Edward T Hurley *1896–1948*	

EWB	Elizabeth W Brain *1898–1902*
FDK	Mrs F D Koehler *1886–90*
FR	Frederick Daniel Rothenbusch *1896–1931*
F.VV	Francis William Vreeland *1900–02*
FW	Fannie Louise Aukland *1881–84*
G.H.	Grace M Hall *1902–05*
HA	Howard Altman *1900–04*
HB	W H Breuer *1881–84*
H.E.W.	Harriet E Wilcox/Willcox *1886–1907*
H.H.	Hattie Horton *1882–84*
HH	
HML	Helen M Lyons *1913–15*
H.R.S.	Harriette Rosemary Strafer *1890–99*

H.W	Harriet (Nettie) Wenderoth *1881–85*
I.B	Irene Bishop *1903–07*
JDM	John D Wareham *1893–1954*
JZE	Josephine E Zettel *1892–1904*
K	Mrs F D Koehler *1886–90*
K.C.M.	Kate C Matchette *1892–94*
KH	Katharine Hickman *1895–1900*
KS	Kataro Shirayamadani *1887–1948*
KVH	Katherine Van Horne *1907–17*
L.A.	Leonore Asbury *1894–1931*
LAF	Laura Ann Fry *1881–91*
L E	Lorinda Epply *1904–48*

LEL	**Laura Lindeman** *1899–1905*	
LNL L.N.L.	**Elizabeth (Lizzie) N Lincoln (née Lingenfelter)** *1892–1931*	
LVB	**Leona Van Briggle** *1899–1904*	
MAD	**Matthew A Daly** *1882–1903*	
MF	**Mattie Foglesong** *1897–1902*	
◇MGD◇	**Mary Grace Denzler** *1913–15*	
(MHM)	**Margaret Helen McDonald** *1913–48*	
M.H.S	**Marian Frances Hastings Smalley** *1899–1902*	
MLN	**Maria Longworth Nichols (later Nichols Storer)** *1880–87*	

MLP	**Mary Louella Perkins** *1886–98*	
MLS	**Maria Longworth Nichols Storer** *1880–87*	
MM	**Marianne Mitchell** *1901–05*	
MN	**Mary M Nourse** *1891–1905*	
MP	**Mary Louella Perkins** *1886–98*	
MR. M.R.	**Marie Rauchfuss** *1897*	
MR	**Martin Rettig** *1883*	
MT	**Mary L Taylor** *1883–85*	
NJH N.J.H.	**Joseph N Hirschfeld** *1882–83*	
O.G.R.	**Olga Geneva Reed (later Reed Pinney)** *1890–1903*	
$P	**Helen Pabodie Stuntz** *1892*	
¶B	**Pauline Peters-Baurer** *1893*	

(PC)	**Patti M Conant** *1915 – late 20s*	
ЯEM	**Ruben Earl Menzel** *1896–1950*	
SA	**Sara Sax** *1896–1931*	
SC	**Sallie (Sara) E Coyne** *1892–1931*	
SJ	**Jeannette Swing** *1900–04*	
SL	**Frederick Sturgis Laurence/ Lawrence** *1895–1904*	
S.M.	**Sadie Markland** *1893–99*	
TOM	**Tom Lunt** *1886–90*	
TS	**Sallie (Sara) Alice Toohey** *1887–1931*	
VBD/	**Virginia B Demarest** *1900–03*	
WHB	**W H Breuer** *1881–84*	
WK.	**William Klemm** *1901*	

SÈVRES

Date letters were used at Sèvres 1753–93 to show the year of manufacture. The letter appeared within or alongside the interlaced 'L' mark. Letters that appear below the mark are usually those of the painter, gilder or potter.

Year marks 1753–93

A	1753	H	1760	O	1767	V	1774	DD	1781	KK	1788
B	1754	I	1761	P	1768	X	1775	EE	1782	LL	1789
C	1755	J	1762	Q	1769	Y	1776	FF	1783	MM	1790
D	1756	K	1763	R	1770	Z	1777	GG	1784	NN	1791
E	1757	L	1764	S	1771	AA	1778	HH	1785	OO	1792
F	1758	M	1765	T	1772	BB	1779	II	1786	PP	1793
G	1759	N	1766	U	1773	CC	1780	JJ	1787		

Marks of painters, gilders & potters at Sèvres

These are alphabetical by initial or monogram, and then by device or other mark. Potters are marked with an asterisk. Dates refer to years active.

Auvillain*
1877–after 1900

Charles-Éloi Asselin
1765–1804

Auguste Lapierre*
1833–43

Auguste Richard
1811–48

Jules Archelais
1865–1902

Alexandre Blanchard
1878–1901

Alexandre Brachard jeune*
1784–92, 1795–99, 1802–27

Louis-Désiré Barré
1846–81

Achille-Louis Bonnuit
1858–62, 1865–94

Antoine-Gabriel Boullemier
1802–42

Adolphe Belet
1881–82

Alphonse-Théodore-Jean Briffaut
1848–90

Alphonse Cieutat*
1894–1928

Coursaget
1881–86

François-Alexandre David
1844–81

Alphonse Dumain*
1884–1928

CERAMICS

Mark	Name	Dates
A.D	Marie-Adélaïde Ducluzeau	1818–48
AD	Pierre-Adolphe Dammouse*	1852–80
AD	François-Alexandre David	1844–81
AD	Alexandre Dubois*	1896–1915
Æ	Anatole Fournier	1878–1926
A L / AL A	Denis Ligué	1881–1911
Al	Jean-Baptiste Allard*	1832–41
A	Armand Lacour*	1895–1911
A	Alexandre Longuet*	1840–76
AM	Alfred Meyer	1858–71
AM	François-Adolphe Moriot	1843–44
ap	Alexandre Percheron*	1827–64

Mark	Name	Dates
R	Antoine-Achille Poupart	1815–48
R	Charles-Alexis Apoil	1851–64
B	Émile Belet	1876–1900
B	Antoine-Louis Bouvrain	1826–48
B	Boulanger père	1754–84
B.	Barré	1773–74, 1776–78
B	Shiridani Baldisseroni	1860–79
B	Barrat l'oncle	1769–91
B.	Jean-Charles-Nicolas Brachard aîné*	1782–1824, or one of the Bougons 1754–1812
B.t	Charles-Marie-Pierre Boitel	1797–1822
B.D	Baudouin père	1750–1800
Bf	Hilaire-François Boullemier fils	1817–55

Mark	Name	Dates
BG	Antoine Bérange	1807–46
Bh	Hilaire-François Boullemier fils	1817–55
Bn	Bulidon	1763–92
Bo	Etienne-Henri Bono*	1754–81
Bt	Louis-Honoré Boquet*	1815–60
Bx	Théodore Buteux	1786–1822
By.	Bailly père	1753–67
Br	Bourdois*	1773–74
C	Claude Couturier	1762–75
C.	Castel	1772–97
B	Charles Barriat	1848–83
CC.	Charles-Louis Constans	1803–40
C	Eugène-Charles Cabau	1847–85

CERAMICS

C.C.	**Abraham Constantin** *1813–48*
CD	**Jean-Charles Develly** *1813–48*
C.D.	**Desnoyers-Chapponet aîné** *1788–1804, 1810–28*
ch.	**Etienne-Jean Chabry fils** *1765–87*
C.L *ch.L*	**Charles Lucas** *1878–1910*
C L.	**Charles-François-Jules Delahaye*** *1818–52*
cm *cm*	**Michel-Gabriel Commelin** *1768–1802*
CN	**Henri-Florentin Chanou jeune*** *1746–79, 1785*
C.P.	**François Capronnier** *1812–19*
cp	**Antoine-Joseph Chappus aîné*** *1761–87*
CR	**Charles Robert*** *1889–1930*

CV	**Charles Villion*** *1894–1941*
D	**Pierre Doré** *1829–65*
D	**Delatre cadet*** *1754–58*
D.D. *D..*	**Dusolle** *1768–74*
D	**Claude-Antoine Tardy** *1755–95*
da	**Danet père*** *1759–after 1780*
DE	**Ernest-Émile Drouet** *1878–1920*
D.F	**Denis Delafosse** *1804–15*
D.F.	**Jean-François Davignon** *1807–15*
DG	**Jean-Charles-Gérard Derichweiler** *1855–84*
D.T	**Gilbert Drouet** *1785–1825*
D.G.	**Mme Catherine Godin** *1806–28*

Dh	**Deutsch** *1803–19*
D.I	**Didier père** *1787–1825* **or fils Charles-Antoine** *1819–48*
D D *D*	**Jules Devicq*** *1881–1928*
D"B	**Mlle Virginie Boullemier** *1814–42*
D.P.	**Claude-Antoine Depérais** *1794–1822*
DR	**Drand** *1764–75, 1780*
DT	**Nicolas Dutanda/Dutenda** *1765–1802*
D	**Taxile Doat** *1879–1905*
Dy	**Charles-Christian-Marie Durosey** *1802–30*
E	**Etienne Latache** *1867–79*
E.	**Edouard Ouint*** *1888–93*

CERAMICS

E·R — **Mme Suzanne-Estelle Apoil** *1865–92*

B — **Eugène-Alexandre Bulot** *1855–83*

E.D. — **Ernest-Émile Drouet** *1878–1920*

E de M — **Mlle de Mauisson** *1862–70*

Ŧ — **Mme Eléonore Escallier** *1874–88*

EF — **Eugène Fromant** *1855–85*

ӾC — **Ambroise-Ernest-Louis Guillemain** *1864–85*

H — **Eugène Hallion** *1870, 1872–74, 1876–93*

EL — **Eugène-Éléonor Leroy** *1855–91*

M — **Mlle Elise Moriot** *1881–86*

P — **Porchon** *1880–84*

ER — **Eugène Richard** *1833–72*

ᴙ — **Émile-Bernard Réjoux** *1858–93*

E.S — **Eugène Simard** *1880–1908*

E.3 — **Jules-Eugène Humbert** *1851–70*

F — **Etienne-Maurice Falconet*** *1757–66*

F — **Fallot** *1773–1790*

Ƒ — **Jean-Baptiste de Fernex*** *c1756*

Ꝼ — **Jean-Joseph Fontaine** *1825–57*

f — **Félix Lévé** *1777–1800*

f f — **Pfeiffer** *1771–1800*

F.B — **François-Antoine Boullemier** *1806–38*

B — **François-Hubert Barbin** *1815–49*

F C — **Alexandre-Frédéric de Courcy** *1865–86*

F.C. — **Mlle Fanny Charrin** *1814–26*

Ꝼ — **Charles Ficquenet** *1864–81*

FF — **Charles Fischbag*** *1834–50*

F.G. / *F.S* — **Frédéric Goupil** *1859–78*

H — **François Hallion** *1865–95*

M — **Maximilien-Ferdinand Mérigot** *1845–72, 1879–84*

P — **Fernand Paillet** *1879–88, 1893*

R — **Joseph-Ferdinand Régnier*** *1826–30, 1836–70*

ꝓ — **François Vaubertrand** *1822–48*

fx fx — **Fumez** *1777–1804*

G — **Jean-Baptiste-Etienne Genest** *1752–89*

211

CERAMICS

G...	**François-Aimé Godin*** *1813–48*	
GB	**Georges Boterel*** *1888–1933*	
GD	**Jean-Charles-Gérard Derichweiller** *1855–84*	
Gd. *GJ.*	**Claude-Charles Gérard** *1771–1824*	
GG.	**Jean Georget** *1801–23*	
GL	**Georges Lebarque*** *1895–1916*	
GE	**Léonard Gébleux** *1883–1928*	
GR	**Alfred-Thompson Gobert** *1849–91*	
GR	**Mme Louise Robert** *1835–40*	
Gt	**Grémont jeune** *1769–75, 1778–81*	
Gu	**Pierre-Louis Ganeau** *1813–31*	
GV GV	**Gustave Vignol** *1881–1909*	

H	**Pierre Houry** *1752–55*	
b	**de Laroche** *1759–1802*	
hc.	**Hericourt** *c1755*	
+HCR	**Henri Renard** *c1881*	
h.J.	**Pierre Huard** *1811–46*	
he.	**Héricourt jeune** *1770–73, 1776–77*	
HF	**Mme Faraguet** *1857–79*	
H. H.	**Henri Laserre*** *1886–1931*	
HP.	**Prévost aîné** *1754–93* **or le second** *1757–97*	
HR	**Henri Robert*** *1889–1933*	
HS	**Sill** *1881–87*	
H	**Henri Trager** *1870–1909*	
HU	**Uhlrich, Henri** *1879–1925*	
h	**Huny** *1785–1800, 1810*	

IC	**Jean-Baptiste Chanou*** *1779–1825*	
J.J	**Jubin** *1772–75*	
J.A	**Jules André** *1840–69*	
J a	**Moïse Jacob-Ber** *1814–48*	
A	**Jules Archelais** *1865–1902*	
JB	**Boileau fils aîné*** *1773–81*	
J.C	**Jules-François Célos** *1865–95*	
J.C.	**Jules Trager** *1847, 1854–73*	
JC.	**Chappuis jeune** *1772–77*	
JD.	**Mme Mère Chanou** *1779–1800*	
È E	**Bernard-Louis-Émile Jardel** *1886–1913*	
E E	**Alexis-Etienne Julienne** *1837–49*	
JR, Jh.R, JhR	**Nicolas-Joseph Richard** *1833–72*	

Mark	Name	Dates
jℏ.	**Henrion aîné**	*1770–84*
ℋL	**Henri-Lucien Lambert**	*1859–99*
JR	**Hyacinthe Régnier***	*1825–63*
J.	**Jules-Eugène Legay***	*1861–95*
JL	**Liance fils aîné***	*1769–1810*
JG	**Léopold-Jules-Joseph Gély***	*1851–89*
j.n.	**Chauveaux fils**	*1771–83*
JQ	**Mme Marie-Victoire Jaquotot/Jacquotot**	*1801–42*
JR	**Julien Risbourg***	*1895–1925*
JR	**Thomas-Jules Roger***	*1852–86*
jt	**Jean-Baptiste Thévenet fils**	*1752–58, 1773–74*
KK	**Charles-Nicolas Dodin**	*1754–1802*
L	**Le Cat***	*1872–after 1900*
L	**Denis Lévé**	*1754–1805*
L	**Auguste Lecterc***	*1897–1911*
L.	**Couturier**	*entered 1783*
B	**Louis-Etienne-Frédéric Blanchard**	*1848–80*
B	**Louis Belet**	*1878–1913*
LB	**Le Bel jeune**	*1773–93*
LB	**Nicolas-Antoine Le Bel**	*1804–45*
LC	**Louis-Joseph Charpentier**	*1852, 1854–79*
Lᵉ	**Jean-Etienne Le Bel aîné**	*1766–75*
LG	**Etienne-Charles Le Guay**	*1778–81, 1783–85, 1808–40*
LG	**Louis Guéneau***	*1885–1924*
LG	**Etienne-Henri Le Guay père**	*1748–49, 1751–96*
LG	**Louis-Antoine Le Grand**	*1776–1817*
lg	**Pierre-Jean-Victor-Amable Langle**	*1837–45*
LGᶜ̃	**Jean-Baptiste-Gabriel Langlacé**	*1807–44*
Li	**Antoine-Mathieu Liance***	*1754–77*
LL LL	**Lécot**	*1773–1802*
LM	**Mirey**	*1788–92*
LM	**Louis Mimard**	*1884–1928*
P	**Léon Peluché**	*1881–1928*
LB	**Mlle Louise Parpette jeune**	*1794–98, 1801–17*
LR	**de Laroche**	*1759–1802*
LR	**J F J Le Riche***	*1757–1801*

CERAMICS

Mark	Name	Dates
M	Moiron	1790–91
M	Jean-Louis Moyez	1818–48
M	Ambroise Michel	1772–80
M	Jean-Louis Morin	1754–87
M	Massy	1779–1803
MA	Achille Mascret	1838–46
Mas	Jean Mascret*	1810–48
MB	Mme Marie-Barbe Bunel	1778–1816
MC	Pierre-Louis Micaud	1795–1834
ME MA	Maugendre*	1879–1887
MLC	Louis Mascret*	1825–64
m. P	Pierre Moyez*	1827–48
M.R	Charles-Raphaël Morin	1805–12
M.R	Denis-Joseph Moreau	1807–15
M	Marc Solon*	1857–71
N	Morin	1880–after 1900
N	François Aloncle	1758–81
NB	Nestor Bestault*	1889–1929
ng.	Nicquet	1764–92
O	Emmanuel Ouint*	1877–89
o.ch	Charles Ouint	1879–86, 1889–90
o g	Jacques-Jean Oger*	1784–1800, 1802–21
M	Optat Milet	1862–79
P	François-Bernard-Louis Pine/Pline	1854–70 or later
P	Perrottin/Perottin	1760–93 or later
P	Philippe Parpette	1755–57, 1773–1806
P.A.	Alexandre-Pau Avisse	1848–84
PB Pb	Philippe Boucot	1785–91
P	Charles Pihan	1879–1928
J F	Pierre Fachard*	1899–1934
P.H.	Philippine aîné	1778–91, 1802–25
P. h.	François Philippine cadet	1783–91,1801–39
P.j.	Pithou jeune	1760–95
P 7. P9.	Jean-Jacques Pierre jeune	1763–1800
PK	Mme de Cour-celles Knip	1808–09,1817–26
P.o	Pierre aîné	1759–75
P P	Mlle Parpette aîné	1788–98
R	Perrenot aîné	1804–09, 1813–15
PR	Pierre Robert	1813–32
P.T.	Nicolas Petit aîné	1756–1806
St.	Pithou aîné	1757–90
R	Pierre Riton	1821–60

214

Mark	Name	Mark	Name	Mark	Name
ᴿᴿ	Sioux aîné *1752–91*	𝒮	Alphonse Sandoz* *1881–1920*	⊡	Claude-Antoine Tardy *1755–95*
R	Nicolas-Joseph Richard *1833–72*	𝒮𝒸	Mlle Sophie, Mme Binet Chanou *1779–98*	E	Etienne Latache *1870–79*
𝒜	Jean-François Robert *1806–43*	𝒮𝒟	Mme Sophie Noualhier *1777–95*	𝒯𝒽𝐹	Théophile Fragonard *1839–69*
𝓡...	Pierre Richard *1815–48*	𝒮𝒮	Louis-Eugène Sieffert *1881–87, 1894–98*	𝐼	Letourneur* *1756–62*
𝓡	Girard *1772–1817*	𝒮.𝒽.	Schrade *1773–75, 1780–86*	.𝐼.	Louis Trager *1888–1934*
𝓡𝓑.	Mme Maqueret *1796–98, 1817–20*	SS	Jacques Sinsson/ Sisson *1795–1846*	𝒫ᵣ: 𝓋ᵣ	Etienne-Joseph Tristan *1837–71, 1879–1882*
𝓡𝓑	Jean-François Robert *1806–43*	SSℓ	Louis Sinsson/ Sisson *1830–34*	V	Paul Villion* *1886–1934*
𝓡	Charles Rémy *1886–97, 1901–28*	SS𝑝	Pierre Sinsson/ Sisson *1818–48*	VD	Pierre-Jean-Baptiste Vandé *1779–1824*
𝓡𝓛 𝓡 𝓽.	Roussel *1758–74*	𝒮. 𝒲. 𝒮𝓌	Jacques-Jose (called Fontaine) Swebach *1803–14*	VD	Vandé père *1753–79*
𝓡ₓ	Denis-Desiré Riocreux *1807–28*	𝒯	Binet *1750–75*	𝒢.𝓉	Mme née Vautrin Gérard *1781–1802*
𝓡ₓ	Isidore Riocreux *1846–49*	𝒯𝒞	Jean-Marie-Dominique Troyon *1801–17*	W	Vavasseur aîné *1753–70*
𝒮	Léon Samson* *1897–1918*			W	Weydinger père *1757–1807*
𝒮	Pierre-Antoine Méreaud aîné *1754–91*				

CERAMICS

W **Joseph Weydinger second fils**
1778–1804, 1807–08, 1811, 1816–24

Hileken
1769–74

Hilken (?)
Before 1800

3V **Pierre Weydinger third fils**
1781–92, 1796–1816

W **Walter**
c1867–70

X **Jacques-François Micaud**
1757–1810

X X **Grison**
1749–71

S **Catrice**
1757–74

XX **Alexandre Rocher**
1758–59

Y **Fouré**
1749, 1754–62

y **Edmé-François Bouillat père**
1758–1810

ૉ **F Bouillat fils**
1800–11

Z. **Joyau**
1766–75

Pierre-Joseph Roisset
1753–95

Apprien-Julien de Choisy
1770–1812

Émile-Victor Martinet
1847–78

Pierre-André Le Guay
1772–1818

Jean-Jacques Anthaume
1752–58

Aubert aîné
1754–58

Claude-Antoine Tardy
1755–95

Cardin
1749–93 or later

Edmé Gomery/ Gommery
1756–58

Léandre 1
1779–85

Armand cadet
1746–88

✝ **Charles Génin**
1756–57

✝ **Philippe and Mlle Xhrouet/Xhrowet/ Secroix**
1750–75

♡ **F Fontelliau**
1753–55

Pajou
1751–59

Émile Renard
1852–82

Boucher
1754–62

Jean-Pierre Ledoux
1758–61

✡ **Jean-Baptiste Bienfait**
1756–after 1770

Fritsch
1763–64

Jean Bouchet
1763–93

Jean-René Dubois
1756–57

Nicolas Sinsson/ Simpson/Sisson
1773–c1800

Mark	Name
❀	**Gautier** *1787–91*
🔔	**Becquet** *1749–50, 1753–65*
🔔	**Pouillot** *1773–78*
⚓	**Charles Buteux aîné** *1756–82*
V	**Mutel** *1754–59, 1765–66, 1771–73*
✗	**Etienne Evans** *1752–1806*
↓	**Yvernel** *1750–59*
❀	**Vincent Taillandier/Tailiandiez** *1753–90*
♪	**Boulanger fils** *1778–81*
♪	**Pierre-François Chevalier** *1755–57*
♪♪	**Thévenet père** *1741–77*
♪♪	**Antoine-Toussaint Cornailles** *1755–1800*
⨆	**Louis-Gabriel Chulot** *1755–1800*

Mark	Name
○	**Sioux jeune** *1752–59*
△	**Capeli** *1746–1800*
△	**Buteux fils cadet** *1773–90*
▲	**Jean-Jacques Dieu** *1777–90, 1794–98, 1801–11*
◈	**Tabary** *1754–55*
✳	**Caton** *1749–98*
✕	**Michel-Barnabé Chauveaux aîné** *1752–88*
✕✕	**Alexandre Rocher** *1758–59*
═	**Bardet** *1751–58*
∴	**Jacques Fontaine** *1752–75, 1778–1807*
≈	**Guillaume Noël** *1755–1804*
⟡	**Raux aîné** *1766–79*
⟡	**Sioux aîné** *1752–91*

Mark	Name
•••	**Charles Tandart jeune** *1756–60* or **Jean-Baptiste Tandart** *1754–1803*
••••	**Théodore** *1765–71 or later*
⌇⌇	**Viellard aîné** *1752–90*
5	**Mongenot** *1754–64*
5.	**Carrié/Carrier** *1752–57*
6	**Bertrand** *1757–74*
6.	**Bertrand** *1750–1800*
9.	**Charles-Nicolas Buteux fils aîné** *1763–1801*
9	**Charles-Louis Méreaud jeune** *1756–79*
2000	**Vincent jeune** *1753–1806*
ℬ	**Louis-Désiré Barré** *1846–81*

CERAMICS

 Horace Bieuville/ Bienville/Bieauville *1879–1925*

Paul* or Henry Brécy* *1881–after 1900*

Alexandre- Frédéric de Courcy *1865–86*

Anatole Fournier *1878–1926*

Léopold-Jules- Joseph Gély *1851–89*

Frédéric Goupil *1859–78*

Alfred Meyer *1858–71*

François Richard *1832–75*

Émile Richard *1867–1900*

Paul-Marie Roussel *1850–71*

Alphonse Sandoz *1881–1920*

Louis-Pierre Schilt *1818–55*

WEDGWOOD DATING CODES

From 1860, as well as its usual name mark, the Wedgwood factory began to use a system of date marking using three impressed letters. The first denotes the month, the second is a potter's mark, and the third indicates the year of manufacture. The system went through three year-mark cycles until 1907 when the system was amended so that the first letter indicated the cycle of year marks in use.

Monthly marks 1860–64

J	January	M	March	Y	May	V	July	S	September	N	November
F	February	A	April	T	June	W	August	O	October	D	December

Monthly marks 1865–1907

J	January	R	March	M	May	L	July	S	September	N	November
F	February	A	April	T	June	W	August	O	October	D	December

First cycle of year marks

O	1860	Q	1862	S	1864	U	1866	W	1868	Y	1870
P	1861	R	1863	T	1865	V	1867	X	1869	Z	1871

Second cycle of year marks

A	1872	E	1876	I	1880	M	1884	Q	1888	U	1892	Y	1896
B	1873	F	1877	J	1881	N	1885	R	1889	V	1893	Z	1897
C	1874	G	1878	K	1882	O	1886	S	1890	W	1894		
D	1875	H	1879	L	1883	P	1887	T	1891	X	1895		

Third cycle of year marks

A	1898	E	1902	I	1906	M	1910	Q	1914	U	1918	Y	1922
B	1899	F	1903	J	1907	N	1911	R	1915	V	1919	Z	1923
C	1900	G	1904	K	1908	O	1912	S	1916	W	1920		
D	1901	H	1905	L	1909	P	1913	T	1917	X	1921		

Fourth cycle of year marks

A	1924	B	1925	C	1926	D	1927	E	1928	F	1929

After 1929 the last two years of the date appear in full.

WORCESTER DATING CODES

In 1862, the Worcester Porcelain Works became known as Royal Worcester. From 1867 a system of dating by year letters was used together with the standard printed mark.

1867–90

A	1867	D	1870	H	1873	L	1876	P	1879	T	1882	W	1885	Z	1888
B	1868	E	1871	I	1874	M	1877	R	1880	U	1883	X	1886	0	1889
C	1869	G	1872	K	1875	N	1878	S	1881	V	1884	Y	1887	a	1890

From 1891, 'Royal Worcester England' was added round the standard mark. From 1892 a dot was added for each year.

1892	one dot added above 'Royal'
1893	two dots, one either side of 'Royal Worcester England'
1894	three dots
1895	four dots
1896	five dots

Dating Codes – Worcester

From 1915 there were 24 dots, some placed below the main mark.

1916	dot replaced by a star below the mark	1917	one dot added to star
		1918	two dots added to star

From 1927 there were 11 dots with the star.

1928	dots and star replaced by a small square	1931	two interlinked circles
		1932	three interlinked circles
1929	small diamond	1933	one dot added to three circles
1930	division sign	1934	two dots added to three circles

From 1941 there were nine dots. Between 1941 and 1948 there were no changes made in year marks.

1949	'V' placed under mark	1955	five dots added to 'W'
1950	'W' placed under mark	1956	'W' is replaced by 'R', dots are added until
1951	one dot added to 'W'		
1952	two dots added to 'W'	1963	13 dots appear with the circled 'R' device
1953	three dots added to 'W'		
1954	four dots added to 'W'		

From 1963 all new patterns feature the year in full.

GLASS

Enamelled cameo glass vase, by Daum

EARLY GLASS

- Much glass produced before the 20thC is unmarked. The exceptions include a few rare, richly decorated pieces, such as a small number of 18thC goblets made by the Beilby family in Newcastle, UK. Some top engravers, such as Jacob Sang and Friedrich Winter, included their monograms in their work. A small number of 19thC exhibition pieces were also signed.

- For more information about early glass marks see Carolus Hartmann's *Glas-Markenlexikon: 1600–1945*, which features thousands of unique marks and signatures.

20thC GLASS

- The McKinley/Taft protectionist tariffs required that all objects imported to the USA between 1891 and 1919 be marked with their manufacturer's name and country of origin. As the American market was essential to the survival of most European glassmakers, most complied with these regulations.

- The emergence of brand marketing (encouraging consumers to pay more for products marketed as particularly luxurious) and the rise of the designer also contributed to much more glass being marked or labelled from the 20thC onwards.

- A very small number of glassworks, including top makers such as Gallé, Lalique, Moser and Venini, chose to mark their wares permanently using acid, moulding or engraving. Pieces signed permanently make up less than 0.01% of the glass produced between 1900 and 1999.

- Due to the high prices achieved by Lalique and Gallé glassware, marks from these companies are often faked. Make sure the quality of the piece is consistent with what you would expect. Another good tip is to look at the area of glass around the signature – on an original piece, this will be of a uniform texture.

- It is also worth bearing in mind that the Lalique and Gallé companies continued to produce glass after the death of René Lalique (1860–1945) and Emile Gallé (1846–1904). Be aware of changes in the mark. After Lalique's death the letter 'R' was dropped from the mark (some forgers carve an 'R' in front of the surname to suggest an earlier piece). After Gallé's death, a star was added to his signature as a sign of respect.

- While some of the makers who used permanent marks signed everything they produced, others only signed certain pieces. For example, at the Mdina glassworks in Malta pieces were only signed if the glassworks were not busy and if the glass designer happened to be present at the right time.

- A small amount of UK glass is embossed with 'Rd' or 'Regd' followed by a number. This allows the owner of the design and the date it was created to be identified.

- Most 20thC glassmakers chose to use either foil or paper labels, rather than indelible marks. Some Scandinavian factories, such as Pukeberg, used marks printed on cellophane from the 1960s. Labels have often been removed or have become damaged by water. It is also worth remembering that some labels may have been applied fraudulently to the work of other companies, but this is a relatively rare occurrence.

- As well as identifying the maker, marks and labels can help with dating as some companies changed their marks over time. Some makers, such as Orrefors, also include the date or a code to the date in their marks.

WHAT IS IN THIS CHAPTER?

The range of material covered in this chapter includes the most common European and American factory marks and designers' marks. The proliferation of factories in the 20thC renders it impossible to include them all, as many of these factories were either short-lived or relatively unimportant.

The marks have been included in the most logical order possible, but this has not always proved to be straightforward. Always check if there is a main factory name present in the mark.

HOW TO FIND YOUR GLASS MARK

The marks and labels in this section are organized in alphabetical order by company name or designer surname.

Anchor Hocking Glass Co.
Lancaster, OH, USA
1906–

This mark 1937–77   *This mark 1977–*

Anfora
Murano, Italy
1970s–
This mark 2004

Ankerglas/Bernsdorf Glassworks
Bernsdorf, Nr. Hoyerswerda, Germany
1872–1987
This mark 1933–65

D'Argental
c1767–
This mark 1919–25

Gabriel Argy-Rousseau (1885–1953)
France
Founded Les Pâtes-de-Verre d'Argy-Rousseau, Paris 1921–32

Arsale / Arsall
Weisswasser, Nr. Rothenburg, Germany
1918–38

Cristalleries de Baccarat
Baccarat, Nr. Lunéville, Nancy, France
1765–

This mark 1930–   *Modern mark*

George Bacchus & Sons
Birmingham, UK
Mid 19thC

Bagley & Co. Ltd.
Knottingley, North Yorkshire, UK
1871–1975

Bohemia Art Glass (BAG)
Vsetín, Czech Republic
1993–

Barbini Vetri Artistici
Murano, Italy
1952–

Barovier & Toso
Murano, Italy
1295–

This mark on: tear-off paper label 'Barovier & Toso Murano Made in Italy' 1936–55; peel-off paper label in red/white 1956–70; peel-off label with company logo 1971–84; or label with text only 1985–.

This mark 1975–

Leopold Bauer (1872–1938)
Czech-born, Austria
Active c1900–20

Adolf Beckert (1884–1929)
Česká Lípa, Bohemia
Active c1900–29

Beránek Glassworks
Škrdlovice, Czech Republic
c1940–

BERANEK

Blenko Glass Co.
Milton, WV, USA
1922–

This label 1930s–c1952

This mark 1970s–

Boda Bruks AB
Boda, Sweden
1864–1976
These marks 1953–
Boda was founded in 1864. In 1964, it formed an alliance with Kosta and Afors. They merged in 1976 and merged with Orrefors in 1990.

Bohemia Glassworks
Poděbrady, Nižbor, Jihlava, Zámecká and Světlá nad Sázavou, all Czechoslovakia
1965–

Chřibská
Czechoslovakia
1960s–80s

Borské Sklo
Chřibská, Nový Bor, Harrachóv, all Czechoslovakia
1953–74
Became Crystalex in 1974

Železný Brod
Czechoslovakia
1960s–80

Boyd's Crystal Art Glass Co.
Cambridge, OH, USA
1978–
This mark 1978–83

British Heat-resisting Glass Co. Ltd. (Phoenix Oven Glass)
Bilston, Staffordshire, UK
1934–70
These marks c1950

Brocard et Fils
France
Active 1865–96
These marks 1867–90

Brockwitz Glasfabrick AG
Sörnewitz, Nr. Meissen, Germany
1903–90
This mark c1928

Burgun, Schverer & Co.
Meisenthal, Lorraine, France
1711–1969
This mark c1890–1900
Post WWII becomes Verrière Meisenthal

Caithness Glass Ltd.
Wick and Perth, Scotland, UK
1961–

This mark c1960s

This mark c1970s

Cambridge Glass Co.
Cambridge, OH, USA
1901–57
This mark 1920–54

Amédée de Caranza
Paris, France
1870–1906

Cenedese Gino e Figlio
Murano, Italy
1946–
This label 1950s–

This mark Orlak range 1929–33

Chance Brothers
Smethwick, Nr. Birmingham, UK
1824–1981

This mark c1950

Mario Cioni
Capraia e Limite, Florence, Italy
1958–

This mark c1970–

PYREX

Corning Glass Works
Corning, NY, USA
1875–
These marks for Pyrex range c1950s

Crystalex
Chřibská, Harrachóv,
Kamenický Šenov, Nový
Bor, all Czechoslovakia
Post-War era

Dartington Glass
Torrington, Devon, UK
1967–

This mark 1967–80s   *This mark 1990s–*

**Dartington
Studio Glass**
Part of
Dartington Glass,
Torrington,
Devon, UK
1998–

Daum
Nancy, France
c1878–

These marks c1895–1900   *This mark 1920s*   *This mark 1990s*

George Davidson & Co. Ltd.
Gateshead, Tyne and Wear, UK
1867–1987

This mark 1880– c1890   *This mark 20thC*

François-Émile Décorchemont (1880–1971)
Conches, Normandy, France
Active 1902–39
Very little glass produced after WWII

Degenhart Crystal Art Glass Co.
Cambridge, OH, USA
1947–78
This mark c1972–78

André Delatte (1887–1953)
Nancy, France
This mark 1919–33

DESPREZ

DESPREZ /
RUE DES RÉCOLETS
NO. 2 A PARIS

Desprez
Paris, France
c1790–1830
This mark c1800

Döbern
Döbern, Nr. Sorau, Germany
1867–
This mark 1955–75

C Dorflinger & Sons
White Mills, PA, USA
c1846–1921

Durobor
Soignies, Belgium
1928–

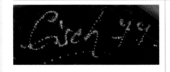

Eda Glasbruk
Värmland, Sweden
1835–1953

Erwin Eisch (b.1927)
Frauenau, Bavaria, Germany
Active 1952–
This mark c1960s–70s

Elme Glasbruk
Almhult, Sweden
1917–70

1917–70   *This mark c1930s*

Ekenäs Glasbruk
Ekenäs, Sweden
1917–76

**Federal
Glass Co.**
Columbus, OH, USA
1900–79

Fenton Art Glass Co.
Williamstown, WV, USA
1905–

This mark 1975–   *This mark 1983–*

**Vittorio Ferro
(b.1932)**
Murano, Italy

Fostoria Glass Co.
Fostoria, OH, then
Moundsville, WV and
Miles, OH, USA
1887–1986

Flygfors Glass
Kalmar County,
Sweden
1888–1979
This mark 1949–79

Emile Gallé (1846–1904)
Nancy, France
Active c1864–1904
This mark 1894–1904

**Cristallerie d'Emile
Gallé**
La Garenne, Nancy,
France
1904–36
This mark 1904–14

Carl Goldberg
Nový Bor, Bohemia
1891–1938

Gral-glashütte GmbH
Dürnau, Göppingen and Leichlingen, Germany
1930–92

Gray-Stan Glass
Battersea, London, UK
1926–36

Greener & Co.

Sunderland, Tyne and Wear, UK
1858–1921
This mark c1885–1900
Company was Henry Greener 1869–95, Greener & Co. 1895–1921, Jobling 1921–75, Corning 1975–

Gullaskruf

Gullaskruf, Småland, Sweden
1893–1995

This mark c1950s

This mark for designer Hugo Gehlin 1927–65

Hadeland Glassverk

Jevnaker, Norway
c1762–

James Hateley

Birmingham, UK
c1880–1920
Trademark registered 1887

Harrachóv Glassworks

Harrachóv, Nový Svet, Bohemia
1630–

This mark c1900–25

This mark 1980s

Thomas G Hawkes & Co.

Corning, NY, USA
1880–1962

Hazel-Atlas Glass Co.

Wheeling, WV, USA
1902–55

A H Heisey & Co.

Newark, OH, USA
1893–1958

Higgins Glass Studio / Michael & Frances Higgins
Riverside, IL, USA
1948–

Holmegaard Glasvaerk
Storstrøm County, Denmark
1825–

This label 1930s

This mark 1940–65

This mark for designer Per Lutken 1942–98

This mark for designer Michael Bang 1973–78

Honesdale Decorating Co.
East Honesdale, PA, USA
c1901–32

Iittala/Iittalan Lasitehdas
Iittala, Finland
1881–

Humppila Glassworks
Finland
1952–86

These labels before 1956

This label 1956–

Imperial Glass Co.
Bellaire, OH, USA
1901–84

This mark 1924–31

These marks 1914–

This mark 1911–32

This mark before 1932

This mark 1977–81

This mark 1981–82

Isle of Wight Studio Glass
Isle of Wight, UK
1973–2013

*This mark for designer
Michael Harris 1972–94*

This mark c1975–82

Auguste Jean
(b.c1830)
Paris, France
Active until 1904

Jeannette
Glass Co.
Jeannette, PA, USA
1898–1983

Jefferson Glass Co.
Follansbee, WV, USA
1900–33

This mark 1907

This mark 1913

Jenaer Glaswerk Schott & Gen
Mainz, Germany
1884–

These marks before 1980

These marks 1981–94

James A Jobling & Co. Ltd.
Sunderland, Tyne and Wear, UK
1921–75
These marks 1921–
See Greener & Co.

Johansfors Glasbruk
Broakulla, Småland, Sweden
1891–1972

Joska
Bavaria, Germany
1961–

King's Lynn Glass
Norfolk, UK
1967–69

Kosta Glasbruk
Sweden
1742–

*This mark for Vicke
Linstrand (1904–1983)
Date code for 1963*

*This mark for Göran
Wärff (1933–)*

**Emil Kromer
or Krommer**
Kamenický Šenov,
Czechoslovakia
Active c1930s–48

**Dominick Labino
(1910–87)**
Toledo, OH, USA
*Active in glass
1963–c1980s
This mark 1973*

René Lalique (1860–1945)
Wingen-sur-Moder, Alsace, France
Active 1902–45
General rule for Lalique marks: 'R Lalique' before 1945

This mark 1926–47

This mark 1920s

This mark 1925–47

Leerdam Glass
The Netherlands
1878–

This mark for Cornelis de Lorm 1916–25

This mark for K P C de Bazel 1916–47

This mark for Andries Dirk Copier 1914–67

This mark for Chris Lebeau 1924–25

This mark for Hendrick P Berlage 1923–34

This mark for Lucienne Block 1928–

This mark for Christian Johannes Lanooy 1919–30

This mark 1970–

This label 1920–

Legras & Cie.
Saint-Denis, Paris, France
1864–1915
Factory reopened as Verreries de Saint-Denis in 1919

This mark Mont Joye 1864–1914

This mark Legras c1910

Wm H Libbey & Sons Co.
Toledo, OH, USA
1888–

This mark 1896–1906

This mark 1906–13

This mark 1919–30

*Mark used 1950s
This mark dated 1955*

Lindshammar Glasbruk
Vetlanda, Sweden
1905–

Liskeard Glass
Cornwall, UK
1970–83

J & L Lobmeyr
Vienna, Austria
1824–
This mark 1925–

Loetz
Klostermühle,
Nr. Rejštejn,
Bohemia
1836–1947

This mark for Loetz client,
Richard, Paris c1920

Les Verreries d'art de Loys Lucha
Paris, France
c1920s

**Jean Luce
(1895–1964)**
La Rochère Glassworks,
France
This mark 1913–30

Kristalunie Maastricht NV
The Netherlands
1902–78

This mark
for Jacob
Rozendaal
1920s–

This mark
before
1972

Målerås Glasbruk AB
Sweden
1890–

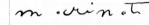

Maurice Marinot (1882–1960)
Troyes, France
Active c1911–37

Giampaolo Martinuzzi (b.1933)
Murano, Italy

Albert Mazoyer
France
Active c1910–45

**McKee & Brothers/
National Glass**
Pittsburgh, PA, USA
1843–1961

Mdina Glass
Malta
1968–
This mark for Michael Harris 1968–72

**Meissener
Bleikristall GmbH**
Germany
1947–

**Meyr's Neffe/
Adolfhütte**
Adolfov nad Vimperk,
Bohemia
1815–1922

John Moncrieff Ltd.
Perth, Scotland, UK
1865–1961
These marks c1924–39

Carlo Moretti SNC
Murano, Italy
1958–

Ludwig Moser
Karlovy Vary,
Bohemia
1857–

This mark c1880–90

This mark c1880–93

This mark 1911–38

This mark 1926–36

This mark c1926–

This mark c1928–30

This mark 1936–38

This mark 1936–91

This mark 1941–45

This mark 1946–

This mark 1992–

Koloman Moser
(1868–1918)
Vienna, Austria
Active c1900–18

Mosser Glass
East Cambridge, OH, USA
1971–
This mark 1980s–

Mount Washington
South Boston, MA, USA
1837–1957

This mark Crown Milano 1880s–

This mark Royal Flemish 1889–

Muller Frères
Lunéville, France
1895–1936

This mark 1895–1914

This mark 1919–

Keith Murray
(1893–1981)

New Zealand, worked in UK
This mark for Royal Brierley Crystal c1934–39

Nason & Moretti
Murano, Italy
c1920s–

This mark 1940s

This mark 1990s

Nazeing Glass Works Ltd.
Broxbourne, Hertfordshire, UK
1928–
This mark 1930s

Northwood & Co./ National Glass
Wheeling, WV, USA
1888–1924
This mark 1908–25

Nuutajärvi Notsjö
Urjala, Finland
1793–

This label before 1953

This label 1953–71, 1977–83, 1987–92

Johann Oertel & Co.
Nový Bor, Bohemia
1869–1945

Okra Glass Studios
Stourbridge, UK
1979–

Orrefors Glasbruk AB
Orrefors, Hovmantorp, Sweden
c1726–

Mark for designer Olle Alberius 1980s

Graal
Technique developed in 1916

**Pallme-König
und Habel**
Košťany, Bohemia
1786–c1945

Cristallerie de Pantin
Paris, France
c1850–c1915
This mark before 1890

Dagobert Peche
(1887–1923)
Austria
Active c1914–23

Bruno Pedrosa (1950–)
Brazil, worked in Murano, Italy
Active 1991–
This mark dated 2003

Peill & Putzler
Glashüttenwerke
GmbH
Düren, Germany
1952–2004
This mark 1970s

Peill & Söhn GmbH
Düren, Germany
1903–52
This label c1920–70

Pilkington
Bros. Ltd.
St Helens and Doncaster,
UK
1826–

PLUS Glasshytta
Frederikstad, Norway
1958–

Glashütte Freiherr
von Poschinger
Frauenau and Zwiesel,
Bavaria, Germany
1568–

Michael Powolny
(1871–1954)
Vienna, Austria
Active 1910–30

Otto Prutscher
(1880–1949)
Vienna, Austria
Active c1908–40s

Pukeberg
Småland, Sweden
1871–

Quezal Art Glass Decorating Co.
Brooklyn, NY, USA
1901–25

Adolf Rasche
Nový Bor, Czechoslovakia
Active c1925

**Raspiller & Cie.
Fenner Glashütte**
Fenne, Germany
1812–1939
This mark c1910–39

Ravenhead Glass
St Helens, Merseyside, UK
1892–

Reijmyre
Reijmyre, Östergötland, Sweden
1810–1926 and 1937–

This mark 1945–70　　*This mark 1970–*

This mark on cameo glass

This mark 1810–

Rheinische Glashütten AG
Köln-Ehrenfeld, Germany
1864–1931

Josef Riedel
Polubny, Bohemia
1888–1958
This label 1925–45

Riedel Glassworks
Kufstein, Austria
1955–

Riihimaki/Riihimäen Lasi Oy Glassworks
Finland
1910–90

This mark 1912–20s

This mark 1930s–60s   *This mark 1970s*

Rimpler GmbH, Kristallglas-manufaktur
Zwiesel, Bavaria, Germany
1920–36, 1946–

Rosenthal AG
Selb, Bavaria, Germany
1879–

This mark 1950s   *This mark 1960s–*

Phil Rosso
Port Vue, PA, USA
1969–
This mark for replica pressed glass

Marius-Ernst Sabino (1878–1961)
Paris, France
Active c1900–39

Saint Clair Glass Works Inc.
Elwood, IN, USA
1938–77
This mark 1940–59

Cristalleries de Saint-Louis
Saint-Louis-lès-Bitche, France
1586–

Salviati & Co.
Murano, Italy
1859–

These marks 1950s–60s

Schneider
Epinay-sur-Seine, France
1908–81

This mark 1920–24

These marks c1920–

**J Schreiber
& Neffen**
Zay-Ugróc, Hungary
c1890s–c1910s

Archimede Seguso (1909–99)
Murano, Italy
Active 1933–99

Seguso Vetri d'Arte
Murano, Italy
1933–
This mark 1960s

Skruf
Kajvägen, Sweden
1897–1977
These marks c1920s

Sowerby
Gateshead, UK
1807–1972
This mark 1876–1930

**Steuben Glass
Works**
Corning, NY, USA
1903–2011

*This mark for designer
Frederick Carder
1903–32*

These marks 1932–

Stevens & Williams
Brierley Hill, England 1776–1847
Became Stevens & Williams in 1847 and Royal Brierley Crystal in 1930

This mark 1927–

This mark c1930–

This mark 1945–

Strathearn Glass Co.
Crieff, Scotland, UK
1965–80

Strömberg
Sweden
1933–79

Stuart & Sons Ltd.
Stourbridge, UK
1881–2001

This mark 1927–45

This mark 1950s

Richard Süssmuth (1900–74)
Silesia, Germany
Active 1915–70
This mark 1920s–30s

Studio Glashyttan I Ahus AD
Åhus, Sweden
1977–

Richard Süssmuth Glashütte
Immenhausen, Germany
1945–96
This mark 1945–

Theresienthaler Kristallglas-manufaktur GmbH
Zwiesel, Germany
1863–
This mark 1920s–30s

Tiffany Glassworks & Decorating Co.
Corona, NY, USA
1892–1920

Tiffany Glassworks & Decorating Co.
Corona, NY, USA
1892–1920

Tiffany Studios
Corona, NY, USA
1902–32
Mark used on lamps

Aureliano Toso
Murano, Italy
1938–
This mark c1956–68

Val St-Lambert
Seraing, Nr. Liège,
Belgium
1826–

This mark c1910

**United States
Glass Co.**
Pittsburgh and
Glassport, PA, USA
1891–1963

This mark 1930s

This label c1930s–40s

Vasart Glass Ltd.
Perth, Scotland, UK
1946–63

Vallérysthal
Vallérysthal/Troisfontaines, Nancy, France
1836–

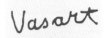

*These marks
1946–63*

Venini e Cie.
Murano, Italy
1925–

This mark 1946–66

This label c1955–59

Vereinigte Lausitzer Glaswerke (VLG)
Weisswasser, Nr. Rothenburg, Germany
1905–45

John Walsh Walsh Ltd. / Soho & Vesta Glassworks
Birmingham, UK
1851–1951
This mark 1930–50

Amalric Walter (1870–1959)
Nancy, France
Active 1903–late 1930s

August Walther & Söhn
Ottendorf, Germany
1936–51

Waterford Crystal/Waterford Glass Ltd.
Waterford, Ireland
1951–

Thomas Webb & Sons
Dennis Park, Stourbridge, UK
1837–1990

This mark 1906–35

This mark on Queen's Burmese ware c1887–1913

This mark c1935–49

T Webb & Corbett Ltd.
Coalburnhill, Stourbridge, UK
1897–1986

This mark 1959–65

This mark c1970

Wedgwood Glass
King's Lynn, Norfolk, UK
1969–92

Westmoreland Glass Co.
Grapeville, PA, USA
1910–84

James Powell & Sons
London, UK
1834–1961

Whitefriars
London, UK
1961–80

This mark 1923–50

This mark 1950–63

This mark 1963–70

Wiener Werkstätte
Vienna, Austria
1903–32

Württembergische Metallwarenfabrik (WMF)
Geislingen, Germany
1853–
Produced glass
1884–1984

L G Wright Glass Co.
New Martinsville, WV, USA
1936–99

These marks 1960s

Železný Brod Glass (ŽBS)
Železný Brod, Czechoslavakia
1960s–80

KOSTA

Kosta Glasbruk uses many marks to identify its glass.

LX	special crystal	MX	machine made	KK	art glass
ELX	semi-crystal	SX	soda glass	U or UNIK	unique pieces
HX	lead crystal	PK	pressed glass		by Göran Wärff

Kosta Boda Art Glass is marked with an article number. This contains six pieces of information: the brand number; the designer's initials; the type of glass; the year of introduction; the product type; and the serial number.

For example, in '8 MBA AT 99 4 001/300': 8 refers to Kosta Boda; MBA to Monica Backström; AT refers to Atelier; 99 is the year of introduction; 4 is the product type; and 001/300 is the serial number.

Designers' marks at Kosta

AEH	Anna Ehrner	GWA	Göran Wärff	UHV	Ulrica Hydman-Vallien
AWA	Ann Wahlström	KEN	Kjell Engman		
BVA	Bertil Vallien	MBA	Monica Backström	W	Göran Wärff
GSA	Gunnel Sahlin	P	Sigurd Persson		

Other Art Glass marks

AT	Atelier (series of 100+ pieces)	ED	Edition (series of less than 60 pieces)	UN	Unique

ORREFORS GLASBRUK AB

Orrefors Glasbruk marks almost all of its pieces with a code, comprising a series of letters and numbers that identify the designer and design date.

- If the letters G, H or L are shown first, followed only by a number, the piece was produced 1917–31.

- If there are two letters (the first representing the designer, the second the glass type), the piece was produced 1926–34.

- If the letters A, E, U or Z (representing glass type) are shown alone, the piece was produced 1935–60.

Glass type codes

A	cut	E	frosted	U	oven finished
AX	cut semi-crystal	F	cut-to-clear	UX	blown semi-crystal
B	jewellery	P	pressed	X	corona
D	lighting	S	graal	Z	lustred

Leading designers' marks at Orrefors

Dates refer to years active at Orrefors. Codes were changed in 1970 (for example, Simon Gate became SG, rather than G). Codes used before 1970 are marked with an asterisk.

A	**Olle Alberius** *1971–93*	**EÖ or F***	**Edvin Öhrström** *1936–57*	**IL**	**Ingeborg Lundin** *1947–71*
B	**Gunnar Cyrén** *1959–70, 1976–*	**G***	**Simon Gate** *1916–45*	**J* or JJ**	**Jan Johansson** *1969–*
D*	**Ingeborg Lundin** *1947–71*	**H***	**Edward Hald** *1917–78*	**L***	**Vicke Lindstrand** *1928–40*
EH	**Edward Hald** *1917–78*	**LH**	**Lars Hellsten** *1972–*	**N* or NL**	**Nils Landberg** *1927–72*

GLASS

P*	Sven Palmqvist *1928–71*	**SP**	Sven Palmqvist *1928–71*	**VL**	Vicke Lindstrand *1928–40*
SG	Simon Gate *1916–45*	**T**	Lars Hellsten *1972–*		

Engravers' marks at Orrefors

Dates refer to years active at Orrefors.

AD	Arthur Diessner *1920–63*	**BH**	Börje Hermansson *1923–41, 1948–65*	**GA**	Gustaf Abels *1915–59*
AK	Ake Hugo Karlsson *1924–45*	**EA**	Ernst Aberg *1947–58*	**GE**	Gösta Elgström *1926–46*
AL	Arne Lindahl *1938–?*	**EG**	Emil Goldman *1923–40*	**GR**	Gustaf Ruud *1920–?*
AN	Axel Nordgren *1927–30*	**EH**	Edit Högsted *1925–31*	**GS**	Gunnar Schultzberg *1926–36*
AR	Arthur Roos *1924–74*	**EP or E–P**	Erich Pohl *1950–75*	**HA**	Harals Axelksson *1946–64*
ARK	Ake R Karlsson *1927–46*	**EW**	Emil Weidlich *1922–29*	**HCn**	Hans Carlsson *1928–32*
ASA	Anders Svensson *1939–?*	**FB**	Fritz Bohman *1923–31*	**HG**	Hakon Gustavsson *1938–61*
B	Birger Gustafsson *1923–27*	**FH**	Fritz Hickisch *1920–c1930*	**HH**	Harold Hansson *1922–28*
BE	Börje Eriksson *1946–?*	**FK**	Folke Karlsson *1923–27*	**Hj**	Hjerton Rydh *1924–39*
BG	Bertil Gustafsson *1926–75*	**FW**	Folke Walwing *1923–27*	**HL**	Hilding Lindahl *1923–27*

GLASS

HR Henry Rydh *1925–43*	**OL** Oskar Landas *1922–70*	**SP** Sven Palmqvist *1928–33*
JA Jan Andersson *1956–62*	**OK** Olle Karlsson *1923–27*	**SP** Sten Pettersson *1922–69*
JR John Rosenstam *1923–62*	**OW** Olle Wigselius *1923–27*	**SW** Sigvard Wulff *1923–41*
KM Karl Müller *1923–27*	**P** Olof Petersson *1925–30*	**ThL** Thure Löfgren *1922–58*
KR Karl Rössler *1923–66*	**PL** Peder Lindahl *1943–65*	**TS** Thutre Schultzberg *1926–56*
LB Liss Bergkvist *1924–59*	**RB** Richard Bayer *1922–27*	**VA** Verner Abrahamsson *1926–46*
L-EN Lars-erik Nilsson *1942–70*	**RB** Ragnar Bergkvist *1921–30*	**WE** Wilhelm Eisert *1920–34*
LjK Ljupce Kocevski *1971–79*	**RH** Reine Hagsted *1925–28*	
NL Nils Landberg *1925–28*	**RP** Rune Pettersson *1940–?*	
O Ove Bjerding *1928–70*	**RR** Ragnar Rosenstam *1921–64*	

Marks on cut décor matt
(numbers increase sequentially from the first shown)

E1–	1926 and earlier	E78–	1928	E140–	1931
E54–	1927	E99–	1929	E182–E201–	1931/32
		E103–	1930		

Marks on polished cut décor
(numbers increase sequentially from the first shown)

A31–	1926 and earlier	A234–	1929	A411–	1933
		A261–	1930	A416–	1934
A197–	1927	A341–	1931		
A205–	1928	A361–	1932		

Marks on engraved glass

1000–1165	1931	1213–1294	1933	1380–1399	1935
1166–1212	1932	1295–1379	1934		

Marks on production glass
(numbers increase sequentially from the first shown)

1400–	1935	2775–	1943	3401–	1953
1521–	1936	2885–	1944	3501–	1954
1692–	1937	2960–	1945	3531–	1955
1910–	1938	3081–	1946/8	3571–	1956
2021–	1939	3121–	1949	3618–	1957
2261–	1940	3171–	1950	3696–	1958
2351–	1941	3221–	1951	3751–	1959
2651–	1942	3351–	1952	3801–	1960

Year letters

A1–A9	1935–43	C1–9	1953–61	E1–9	1971–79
B1–9	1944–52	D1–9	1962–70	F1–9	1980–88 etc

Numbers used on early Graal pieces (1916–30)
(numbers increase sequentially from the first shown)

1	1916	1064–	1921	2082–99 and 3000–	1926
102–	1917	1090–99 and 2000–	1922	3065–	1927
522–	1918	2004–	1923	3077–	1928
739–	1919	2014–	1924	3245–	1929
869–	1920	2032–	1925	3259–3292	1930

Numbers used on later Graal pieces (1937–81)
(numbers increase sequentially from the first shown, letters are constant throughout range)

10–	1937	438D–	1952	101B–251B	1967
165–	1938	1836D–	1953	Nil	1968
347–	1939	2867D– 3000D and 200H–1386H	1954	100D–135D	1969
504–	1940			100E–364E	1970
552–	1941	1387K–2547K	1955	101F–359F	1971
795–	1942	101L–	1956	100G–311G	1972
1214–	1943	1267L–1276L and 101M–1294M	1957	100E3–267E3	1973
1404–	1944			101E4–452E4	1974
1935–	1945	100N–1204N	1958	101E5–462E5	1975
2356–	1946	100O–1334O	1959	100E6–370E6	1976
2825–99 and 300B–	1947	100P–	1960	100E7–327E7	1977
651B–	1948	961P–963P and 100R–733R	1961	100E8–258E8	1978
1661B–1699B and 200C–	1949			100E9–183E9	1979
		101S–695S	1962	100F1–201F1	1980
870C–	1950	101T–426T	1963	100F2–219F2	1981
1915C– 2114C, 2015C–29C, 2030C– 2099C and 200D–	1951	101V–342V	1964		
		101A–	1965		
		344A–633A	1966		

COSTUME JEWELLERY

Crown brooch, by Trifari

- Many pieces of costume jewellery are marked with the designer's and/or manufacturer's name.

- Marks can help with dating as over time companies often changed marks.

- Some companies included the date of manufacture within the mark. From 1955, costume jewellery designs could be copyrighted, so © indicates that a piece was made after that date.

- Stamped patent numbers can be used to research the date of the design and other information, such as the name of the designer.

- The marks in this section are organized in alphabetical order by the name of the company. If a company takes its name from that of an individual, for example Miriam Haskell, the surname has been used.

Art
New York, NY, USA
1940s–c1970
This mark 1955–

Balenciaga
Paris, France
c1970–

Balmain
Paris, France
c1950–

McClelland Barclay
Providence, RI, USA
c1935–43

Beaujewels
USA
c1950–70s

Ben-Amun
New York, NY, USA
1977–

Marcel Boucher
New York, NY, USA
1937–early 1970s
This mark 1955–

Hanna Bernhard
Paris, France
c1990–

BSK
New York,
NY, USA
c1948–80
*This mark
1955–*

Butler & Wilson
London, UK
c1970–

Cadoro Inc.
New York, NY, USA
1954–87
This mark 1955–

Hattie Carnegie
New York, NY, USA
c1950–79
This mark 1955–

Joan Castle
Los Angeles, CA, USA
This mark 1950s

Alice Caviness
Long Island, NY, USA
c1945–c2000

Chanel
Paris, France
1912–
This mark 1925–

Chanel Novelty Co.
New York, NY, USA
1930s–40s

Ciner
New York, NY, USA
1892–
This mark 1931–

Coppola e Toppo
Milan, Italy
Late 1940s–86

Coro
Providence, RI, USA
c1938–79

Coro Duette c1931–50s

This mark c1938–c1955

Robert DeMario
New York, NY, USA
1945–65

Carol Dauplaise
New York, NY, USA
1978–

De Luxe
New York, NY, USA
c2000–

Déposé
French mark for a
registered design
This mark c1900–

Christian Dior
Paris, France
1947–

This mark c1955–c2000

This mark for Mitchel Maer
1950s

This mark 1958

**DRGM (Deutsches
Reichs-
gebrauchsmuster)**
German patent mark
1891–early 1950s

Eisenberg Original
Chicago, IL, USA
c1930–
This mark c1935–45

Eugene
New York, NY, USA
c1950–60

Fabrice
Paris, France
c1960–

Theodor Fahrner
Pforzheim, Germany
1855–1979
This mark c1900–

Fendi
Rome, Italy
1972–

Florenza
New York, NY, USA
c1950–81
This mark 1955–

Givenchy
Paris, France
1952–

Goldette
New York, NY,
USA
c1958–late 1970s

Grosse
Pforzheim, Germany
c1940–55
This mark dated 1953

Stanley Hagler
New York, NY, USA
Late 1950s–96
This mark 1983–

Har
New York, NY, USA
1950s–60s
This mark 1955–

Miriam Haskell
New York, NY, USA
1924–

This mark 1950s–

This mark 1940s–50s

Hobé
New York, NY, USA
1927–late 1990s
This mark 1958–83

Hollycraft
New York, NY, USA
1948–mid 1970s

Jacob Hull
Jutland, Denmark
1970s–93

George Hunt
Birmingham, UK
c1920–60
This mark dated 1937

Iradj Moini
New York, NY, USA
1989–

Jewelcraft
Providence, RI, USA
1920–50s

Jomaz
New York, NY, USA
1946–81

Jonne (House of Schrager)
New York, NY, USA
c1950–60

Joseff of Hollywood
Los Angeles, CA, USA
1935–
These marks 1938–

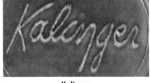

Kalinger
Paris, France
1986–90s

Kalo Shop
Chicago, IL, USA
1900–70

Kenzo
Paris, France
1970–

Alexis Kirk
New York, NY, USA
1970s–2010

Anne Klein
New York, NY, USA
1968–

Kramer
New York, NY,
USA
1943–80

KTF (Trifari)
New York, NY, USA
1918–
This mark dated 1935–

**Christian
Lacroix**
Paris, France
c1989–2009

Lalique
Paris, France
1881–
This mark c1920s

Kenneth J Lane
New York, NY, USA
1963–

Lanvin
Paris, France
1909–

Guy Laroche
Paris, France
1957–

Leru
New York, NY, USA
c1950–60s
This mark 1955–

Les Bernard
New York, NY, USA
c1962–96

Lisner
New York, NY, USA
c1904–c1985
This mark 1955–

Marboux (Marcel Boucher)
New York, NY, USA
1937–60s
This mark 1955–

Marvella
New York, NY and
Philadelphia, PA, USA
1911–
This mark 1955–

Matisse
Los Angeles, CA, USA
1952–64
This mark 1955–

Mazer
Philadelphia, PA and New York, NY, USA
1927–81
This mark 1946–

Mimi di N
New York, NY, USA
1960s–
Marks dated c1970–
This mark dated 1976

Monet
Providence, RI, USA
1922–99
This mark 1955–

Napier
Meridien, CT, USA
1922–99
This mark 1955–

Jean Patou
Paris, France
1919–87
This mark c1925–

Pennino
New York, NY, USA
1927–61

Paloma Picasso
Paris, France
1960–

Lucien Piccard
New York, NY, USA
c1944–

Poggi
Paris, France
1976–

**JMP Paris
(Jean-Marie Poinot)**
Paris, France
1975–

Potter Studio
Chicago, IL, USA
1915–28

**Princess Helietta
Caracciolo**
Rome, Italy
c1970–

**Rebajes
(Francisco Rebajes
1906–90)**
New York, NY, USA
c1932–67

Regency
New York, NY, USA
c1950–70

Réja
New York, NY, USA
c1940–54

Renoir
Los Angeles, CA,
USA
1946–64

Robért
New York, NY, USA
1942–79

Nina Ricci
Paris, France
c1960s–

This mark early 1940s

This mark 1955–

Rochas
Paris, France
1925–

Yves Saint Laurent
Paris, France
c1960–

Schiaparelli
Paris, France and New York, NY, USA
1931–73
This mark for US-made jewellery 1949–60s

Schreiner
New York, NY, USA
1939–77

Selini (Selro)
New York, NY, USA
Late 1940s–75
This mark 1955–60s

Sphinx
London, UK
c1950–c2000

Elizabeth Taylor for Avon
New York, NY, USA
1993–97

Trifari
New York, NY, USA
1918–

This mark 1955–

This mark for Kunio Matsumoto 1970s

Vargas
Providence, RI, USA
1945–c1996

Vendôme (Coro)
Providence, RI, USA
1944–79

Lawrence (Larry) Vrba
New York, NY, USA
1983–

Weiss
New York, NY, USA
1942–71
This mark 1955–

Vivienne Westwood
London, UK
c1980–

Whiting & Davis
Providence, RI, USA
1876–
This mark 1907–

Carlo Zini
Milan, Italy
c1980–

DOLLS, TEDDIES & TOYS

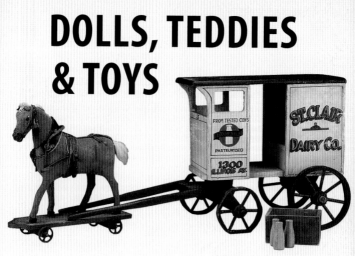

St Clair Dairy Co. milk wagon, by Schoenhut

- Many bisque dolls are marked on the back of the head under the wig. Shoulder-head dolls are often marked on the back of the shoulder and cloth dolls on the foot.

- Doll marks can often reveal the name of the maker and their country of origin as well as the doll's mould number, size and trademark.

- Teddy bears sometimes have labels sewn on to the footpad or stitched into the side seam, but many labels have been lost or removed. Other bears, such as those by famous German company Steiff, have ear buttons.

- Most toys made after 1920 have some form of identification on them, usually a trademark or country of origin.

- The marks in this section are organized in alphabetical order by company name. If a company takes its name from that of an individual, for example Armand Marseille, the surname has been used.

Amanda Jane
UK
1952–2007

Annalee Mobilitee Dolls Inc.
Meredith, NH, USA
Mid 1950s–

ARRANBEE
DOLL Cº

Arranbee Doll Co.
New York, NY, USA
1922–61

Bähr & Pröschild
Ohrdruf, Germany
1871–1925

B & P
320-10
dep

This mark 1895–c1900

678
4
BP

Made in
Germany

This mark 1919–

Barbie (Mattel Inc.)
El Segundo, CA, USA
1959–

ING
EAUTY
ABY.

Gebrüder Bing
Nuremberg, Bavaria, Germany
1863–1932
This mark 1919–

BRU Jⁿᵉ et Cⁱᵉ Nº 1
DEPOSE

Bru Jeune et Cie.
Paris, France
1866–99
Merged with SFBJ in 1899

PAWTUCKET, R.I
MADE IN U.S.A.

Martha Jenks Chase
Pawtucket, RI, USA
1880–1925

Dean's Rag Book Co.
London, UK
1903–

Gaultier Frères
Charenten and St Maurice, France
1860–99 Merged with SFBJ in 1899

effanbee

Effanbee
New York and Kingston, NY, USA
1912–
This mark registered 1913

This mark c1877–c1918

*This mark used on bodies with
Gaultier heads until c1918*

E. GESLAND
B^TE S. G. D. G.
PARIS

The Gesland Co.
Paris, France
1860–1928

William Goebel
Oeslau-Rödental, Germany
1871–

**GREINER'S
PATENT HEADS.
No. 0.
Pat. March 30th, '58.**

Ludwig Greiner
Philadelphia, PA, USA
1840–84

Germany

HEINRICH HANDWERCK
SIMON & HALBIG

Heinrich Handwerck
Waltershausen, Germany
1855–1902
This mark used on heads designed by Heinrich Handwerck and produced by Simon & Halbig

Max Handwerck
Waltershausen, Germany
c1900–30

Ernst Heubach
Köppelsdorf, Thuringia, Germany
Active 1887–c1930

This mark used on early shoulder-head dolls

This mark 1887–c1930

This mark 1890s–

Gebrüder Heubach
Thuringia, Germany
c1843–1940
Produced dolls from 1910–

Edward Imeson Horsman
New York, NY, USA
1865–1920s
This mark c1900–

Maison Huret
Paris, France
c1850–1920

Ideal Novelty & Toy Co.
Brooklyn, NY, USA
1903–82

Jumeau
Paris and Montreuil-sous-Bois, France
1842–99 Merged with SFBJ in 1899

This mark before 1878

This mark 1878–

This mark 1885–

This mark used on the most expensive Jumeau dolls

Kämmer & Reinhardt
Waltershausen, Germany
1886–1920s

Kestner & Co.
Waltershausen, Germany
1805–1930

These marks 1918–

Dolls

Kewpies

1912–
Designed by American Rose O'Neill, licensed to George Borgfeldt & Co.
Made in Germany (some by Kestner) and the USA

This Rose Art USA mark c1960s

Leopold Lambert
Paris, France
c1888–1923

Armand Marseille

Köppelsdorf, Thuringia, Germany
1884–late 1930s

560
Germany
A. 2 M.
D·R·G·M·

Made in Germany
Armand Marseille.
560a
A 7/0 M
D.R.M.R 238

This mark registered in 1893   *This mark 1900–*   *This mark 1909–*   *This mark 1910–*

Montanari
13 Charles St
Soho Sqr
London

Charles Marsh
London, UK
c1878–94

Herbert John Meech
London, UK
1865–1917

Montanari
London, UK
c1851–70s

272

Ch. Motschmann
Sonneberg, Brandenburg,
Germany
c1850–60

Gebrüder Ohlhaver
Sonneberg, Brandenburg, Germany
1912–c1930
This trademark c1913–

R.4.D
R 5/0 D

Rabery & Delphieu
Paris, France
c1856–1930

**Marie Antoinette
Leontine Rohmer**
Paris, France
c1859–80

A Schoenhut & Co.
Philadelphia, PA, USA
1872–c1925

Simon & Halbig
Gräfenhain, Nr. Ohrdruf, Germany
1839–1920

**Société Française de Fabrication de
Bébés et Jouets (SFBJ)**
1899–1950
*Association of prominent French dollmakers formed in
response to German competition*

A N Théroude
Paris, France
1837–95

Izannah F Walker
Central Falls, RI, USA
c1840–86
This mark 1873–

Norah Wellings
Wellington, Shropshire, UK
1926–59

Teddy Bears

Gebrüder Bing
Nuremberg, Baravia, Germany
1863–1932

This mark 1908–

This label 1919–27

This label 1927–32

Wendy Boston
South Wales, UK
1945–76
This label before 1960

Bruin Manufacturing Co. (BMC)
New York, NY, USA
1907–09

Chad Valley
Harborne, Birmingham, UK
1920–

This button c1930–39

This button 1930s

This label 1930s

This label 1953–

This label c1955

This label late 1950s

Chiltern
Chesham, Buckinghamshire, UK
1908–67

This label 1950s

This label used for a short time after 1967 following company's takeover by Chad Valley

Dean's Rag Book Co.
London, UK
1903–

This button c1930

This mark 1930s

This label 1920s–55

This label 1956–80s

Farnell & Co.
London, UK
1840–1968

Ealon Toys
London, UK
1914–early 1950s
This label c1930

This label 1925–45

This label 1959–68

Gebrüder Hermann
Hirschaid, Germany
1907–

This mark c2000

This label c2000

House of Nisbet
Weston-super-Mare, later Winscombe, UK
1953–89
This label 1987–
The company was acquired by US firm Dakin in 1989

Merrythought
Colbrookdale, Shropshire, UK
1930–

This label 1930s–57

This button 1930s

This label c1930

This label 1957–91
'REGD DESIGN' used in
first year of manufacture

This label 1957–91

Jopi
Nuremberg, Germany
1910–late 1950s

This label 1930s–50s

This label 1950s

Peacock Bros.
London, UK
1904–39
This label 1931–39

Marcel Pintel
Paris, France
c1918–76
This label c1930s

Pixie Toys
Stourbridge, UK
1930s–62
This label 1940s

Schuco (Schreyer & Co.)
Nuremberg, Germany
1912–77

This mark 1921–

This mark 1950–

Steiff
Giengen, Württemberg, Germany
1877–
First bear designed in 1902

This button 1904–05

This button 1904–05

This button 1905–50s
This label 1908–

This button in various sizes
and also in brass 1905–50s

This button 1948-50

This button 1950-52

This label 1952–72 and
on replica bears 1983–

This button 1952-72

This button and label
1952–72

This button and label
1960s-70s

This label 1970–

This button in various
forms 1980s–

This button and label
c2000

277

Strunz Toys
Nuremberg, Bavaria,
Germany
1902–14
This button and
label 1908–

Tara Toys (Erris Toys before 1953)
Elly Bay, County Mayo, Republic of Ireland
1938–79

Toys & Games

Alps Shoji Ltd.
Tokyo, Japan
1948–70s
Became an electronic
goods manufacturer
in 1970s

Bassett-Lowke
Northampton, UK
1899–

**Bell Toys
& Games Ltd.**
London, UK
1919–unknown

Gebrüder Bing
Nuremberg, Bavaria, Germany
1863–1932

Bird & Sons
Birmingham, UK
1870s–unknown

Bowman Models Ltd.
Dereham, Norfolk
1928–36
Luton, Bedfordshire
c1945–50

William Britains Ltd.
London, UK
1847–
Became part of First Gear
in 2005

Karl Bub
Nuremberg, Bavaria, Germany
1851–1966
Company revived 2006

Bühler
Germany
1860–unknown

Ettore Cardini Co.
Italy
1922–28

Georges Carette & Cie.
Nuremberg, Bavaria, Germany
1886–1917

Chad Valley
Harborne, Birmingham, UK
1920–

Combex
Peterborough, UK
1946–80
Taken over by Dunbee
Ltd. in 1960

**Corgi (formerly
part of Mettoy)**
Northampton, UK
1956–

Dinky Toys
Liverpool, UK
1934–c1980

This mark Dinky Dublo 1957–64

Johann Distler & Co.
Nuremberg, Bavaria, Germany
c1900–62

Doll & Cie.
Nuremberg, Bavaria, Germany
1898–1938

Dunbee-Combex-Marx
London, UK
1962–80

Hans Eberl
Nuremberg, Bavaria, Germany
c1900–29

Gebrüder Einfalt
Nuremberg, Bavaria, Germany
1922–c1979
Became Technofix in 1935

J Falk
Nuremberg, Bavaria, Germany
c1897–c1940

H Fischer & Co.
Nuremberg, Bavaria, Germany
c1908–32

Fisher-Price
East Aurora, NY, USA
1930–

Gebrüder Fleischmann
Nuremberg, Bavaria, Germany
1887–

Fuchs & Co.
Nuremberg, Bavaria, later Zirndorf, Germany
1919–

DOLLS, TEDDIES & TOYS

Girard Model Works Inc.
Girard, PA, USA
1919–35
Became Girard Manufacturing Co. in 1922
Became The Toy Works 1935–75

**Industrias
Geyper SA**
Valencia, Spain
1957–

**Greppert & Kelch /
Gundka-Werke**
Brandenburg, Germany
1912–30

„Perplex‡

Günthermann
Nuremberg, Germany
1887–1965

E Hausmann
Nuremberg, Bavaria,
Germany
c1910–30

O & M Hausser / Elastolin
Ludwigsburg, Württemberg, Germany
1904–83

Georg Heyde
Dresden, Germany
1872–1945

Höffler
Fürth, Germany
1938–47

**Hubley
Manufacturing Co.**
Lancaster, PA, USA
1898–1942

**Ichiko Kogyo
Co. Ltd.**
Tokyo, Japan
c1950–70

DOLLS, TEDDIES & TOYS

Issmayer
Nuremberg, Germany
1861–1932

Kohner Bros Inc.
New York, NY, USA
c1940–70
Became part of General Foods in 1969

Köhnstam
Fürth, Bavaria, Germany
c1875–1959

Ernst Lehmann & Co.
Brandenburg, Germany
1881–c1945
Nuremberg, Baravia, Germany
1951–

Lineol
Brandenburg, Germany
1905–
Dresden, Germany
1949–

Lionel Manufacturing Company
NY and NJ, USA
1900–

Mangold
Fürth, Bavaria, Germany
1882–c1990s

Märklin
Göppingen, Baden-Württemberg, Germany
1859–

Fernand Martin
Paris, France
c1878–c1920
Taken over by Victor Bonnet et Cie. in the 1920s

Louis Marx & Co.
New York, NY, USA
1920–82

Meccano
Liverpool, UK
1901–

Mettoy Co. Ltd.
Northampton, UK
1933–83

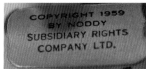

Noddy Subsidiary Rights Co. Ltd.
London, UK
1952–94

Ernst Plank
Nuremberg, Bavaria,
Germany
1866–1930

Timpo Toys
London and Shotts,
North Lanarkshire, UK
1938–78

Tri-ang
Merton, London, UK
1919–71
This mark registered 1924

Trix
Nuremberg, Bavaria, Germany
c1930–73
*A subsidiary company was established in 1935
in the UK*

Index

Index